DOBERMAN
AND
DOBERMAN PINSCHER

Doberman Pinscher
Total Guide

DOBERMANS, DOBERMAN BREEDERS, DOBERMAN PINSCHER PUPPIES
TO DOBERMAN DOGS, DOBERMAN TRAINING, DOBERMAN DISCIPLINE,
DOBERMAN HEALTH, DOBERMAN BREEDING, CARE, AND MORE!

By Mark Manfield
© DYM Worldwide Publishers

DYM Worldwide Publishers

ISBN: 978-1-911355-82-3

for, the websites being temporarily or being removed from the Internet. The accuracy and completeness of the information provided herein, and opinions stated herein are not guaranteed or warranted to produce any particular results, and the advice or strategies, contained herein may not be suitable for every individual. The author, publisher, distributors, and/or affiliates shall not be liable for any loss incurred as a consequence of the use and application, directly or indirectly of any information presented in this work. This publication is designed to provide information in regard to the subject matter covered. The information included in this book has been compiled to give an overview of the topics covered. The information contained in this book has been compiled to provide an overview of the subject. It is not intended as medical advice and should not be construed as such. For a firm diagnosis of any medical conditions, you should consult a doctor or veterinarian (as related to animal health). The writer, publisher, distributors, and/or affiliates of this work are not responsible for any damages or negative consequences following any of the treatments or methods highlighted in this book. Website links are for informational purposes only and should not be seen as a personal endorsement; the same applies to any products or services mentioned in this work. The reader should also be aware that although the web links included were correct at the time of writing they may become out of date in the future. Any pricing or currency exchange rate information was accurate at the time of writing but may become out of date in the future. The Author, Publisher, distributors, and/or affiliates assume no responsibility for pricing and currency exchange rates mentioned within this work.

Table of Contents

CHAPTER 1

Introducing the Doberman Pinscher

A lert and watchful, the mighty Doberman Pinscher may look intimidating, but underneath that serious exterior lives a big teddy bear. Although they were bred to be menacing guard dogs, the Doberman has made the transition from fierce protectorate to the loveable family dog. When well-socialized from an early age and trained to be obedient, the Doberman Pinscher becomes a wonderful dog to have around children. You will quickly see that the Doberman's powerful and dangerous outward appearance does not reflect the playful, happy personality of the breed. Proud owners of Doberman Pinschers soon abandon adjectives like "menacing" and "intimidating" in favor of words like "calm," "obedient," "shy," "smart," and "athletic."

It is easy to spot a Doberman. Their erect ears give them a perpetually alert appearance and their broad, athletic chest and smooth coat shows off their muscular build. The Doberman is a quintessential guard dog and will faithfully protect his family. He will join you on a run around the park, or a swim at the lake, and will love to have you toss a ball or Frisbee to him whenever you can. Dobermans are surprisingly shy and reserved. They have a personal space bubble around them, and they don't like to let strangers in. It is different with their family though. They are affectionate and cuddly towards people they know well.

Ever vigil, the Doberman is a wonderful companion dog and faithful watchdog.

This Doberman Pinscher guidebook is intended to help you learn more about Dobermans, so you can determine if this is the dog breed for you and your family. Dobermans bring some unique qualities to their owners and will quickly become an important member of the family. In this Doberman Pinscher handbook, we will discuss breed-specific information about training, feeding, and keeping your Doberman healthy and happy. You will also see information about finding a reputable Doberman breeder, caring for Doberman puppies, puppy-proofing your home, and even how to address changes that arise as your Doberman enters his golden years.

With your increased Doberman Pinscher savvy, you will gain insight into why the Doberman has remained one of the more popular dog breeds worldwide. We will showcase the unique characteristics of this devoted and good-natured pooch to prove that you can't judge a dog's heart from its cover.

CHAPTER 2

What is the History of the Doberman Pinscher

The Doberman Pinscher has enjoyed an interesting history, yet one that is shrouded in mystery. We don't know, to this day, the exact canine make-up for the Doberman, but we do know that this dog was bred to fill a distinct niche…that of a guard dog.

How and Why Were Dobermans Developed?

Karl Friedrich Louis Doberman (whose last name is sometimes spelled "Dobermann") held two important positions in the town of Apolda, in Thüringen, Germany, in the late 1800s. He served as a tax collector, and he ran the local dog pound. Tax collecting in late nineteenth century Germany was a dangerous profession and Herr Doberman regularly traveled through questionable areas, known for harboring bandits and criminals, while carrying large sums of cash. He soon devised a way to protect himself that involved his second job as kennel keeper at the Apolda dog shelter. With many different breeds at his disposal, Herr Doberman began a breeding program with the goal of creating a breed of dog that was intimidating in appearance, aggressive and protective, as well as obedient and intelligent. His end result was the Doberman Pinscher, a mighty, formidable, and loyal dog that would take his name.

Bred to be a protector and guard, the Doberman Pinscher is a hard-working dog.

Herr Doberman, unfortunately, was a better dog breeder than he was record-keeper. He did not keep good records of his dog breeding activity, so we do not know what breeds comprise the Doberman Pinscher's background. We can only speculate. Most experts believe that the Doberman was developed from the smooth-coated German Pinscher, Rottweiler, and the Black and Tan Terrier, but the Doberman could also contain some Greyhound, Weimaraner, Beauceron, and Manchester Terrier, although exact ratios cannot be determined. Herr Doberman was pleased with the outcome of his guard dog, which he described as the ideal combination of loyalty, endurance, speed, intelligence, ferocity, and strength.

The Doberman Pinscher breed was most likely stable by the 1890s. When Herr Doberman passed away in 1894, the German Kennel Club officially named the breed in his honor, although they did not officially recognize the breed until 1900. Subsequent dog breeders, primarily Otto Goeller and Philip Greunig, continued work on the dog breed, giving us the Doberman that is so recognizable today.

How Did the Doberman Pinscher Get Its Name?

It is easy to see where the Doberman name originated, but the Pinscher part proved to be more problematic. By the mid-1900s, the German Kennel Club dropped the word Pinscher from the dog breed's name, stating that it was misleading. "Pinscher" means "terrier" in German, and the Doberman breed was not considered to be a terrier. In fact, Dobermans are members of the working class of dogs. The British Kennel Club followed suit and removed the Pinscher term a few years after the Germans. Canada and the United States are the only countries that still use the original name of Doberman Pinscher.

Dobermans quickly spread throughout Europe and, by the 1920s, they could be found as far as South Africa, Russia, and the United States. The Dobermans proved to be smart, athletic, and highly trainable and they quickly transitioned from guard dogs to working with the military and police forces. They are imposing enough to track criminals and do search and rescue, yet gentle enough to work as therapy dogs and leader dogs for the sight impaired.

The Doberman as War Dogs

When the United States Marine Corps occupied Europe during World War II, the Marines were introduced to the Doberman dogs. They were so taken with the strong and loyal dogs that they adopted the Doberman Pinscher breed, then known as Devil Dogs, as their official war dog. The War Dogs were ever-vigil and protective guard dogs. In one well-documented story, a Doberman named Cappy, alerted his unit of approaching Japanese soldiers in Guam, saving the lives of 250 United States Marines. Later, Cappy was killed by a Japanese grenade on July 23, 1944, making him the first canine casualty of the war. He was the first animal buried in the War Dog Cemetery, located at the U.S. Naval Base on Guam. In fact, a bronze likeness of Cappy keeps watch from atop the World War II War Dog Memorial. The statue, created by Susan Bahary and dedicated in 1994, is titled, "Always Faithful."

Dobermans have proven to be an asset to police and military units.

Dobermans in America

Even before World War II, Dobermans were gaining popularity in the United States. The American Kennel Club officially recognized the breed in 1908. In 1921, George Earle III founded the Doberman Pinscher Club of America. In the 1970s, Dobermans ranked in the top five most popular dog breeds in North America, but they since dropped in the rankings. Today, they are found in the number 12 position. Among the reasons for this could be the portrayal of Dobermans as frighteningly aggressive guard dogs in popular movies. A well-known quote by Cesar Milan, the Dog Whisper, demonstrates this: "In the 70s, they blamed Dobermans. In the 80s, they blamed German Shepherds. In the 90s, they blamed Rottweilers. Now they blame Pit Bulls. When will they blame humans?" But, it could also be that Dobermans were simply usurped by the increased popularity of other breeds, such as the Cocker Spaniel, Shar-Pei, and the Golden Retriever.

Today, the Doberman is still associated with guard dogs and police dogs. They are one of the most recognizable of all dog breeds, thanks to his ever-alert, erect ears, and sleek athletic build. Doberman owners across the globe will attest that beneath that formidable exterior beats the heart of a lovable and loyal companion that is calm, intelligent, and playful.

CHAPTER 3

Is the Doberman Pinscher the Right Dog for Me?

Dobermans are intimidating animals. Their imposing physique and unfounded reputation are often enough to dissuade potential Doberman owners. Yet there is more to this impressive dog than meets the eye. They can be wonderful family dogs and true companions. Dobermans do, however, require a lot from their owners. Before you make the decision to get a Doberman Pinscher, you should understand as much as you can about this unique breed.

What Are Doberman Pinschers Like as Pets?

If they have been properly socialized and trained from puppyhood, Doberman Pinschers are sweet and loving pets who are good with children. They are people-pets, but often, they will bond with only one family member. Dobermans are great for active families because they require lots of exercise, whether it is a jog through the neighborhood or chasing a ball around the backyard. They are energetic and athletic, and they may get a bit cranky if they aren't exercised enough. They also need mental stimulation. The superb intelligence of the Doberman breed makes them easy to train with positive reinforcement, and their natural guard dog tendencies mean they will be a good protector of the family. Even though he may look like an imposing watchdog, the Doberman is just as likely to cuddle up at your feet or try to take over your bed. He is really a big ol' softie.

Dobermans may look imposing, but they are really just big cuddlers.

What is the Doberman Pinscher Temperament?

Obviously, each Doberman Pinscher has his own distinct personality. While most Doberman dogs are somewhat reserved and shy, some can be quite outgoing. As a whole, Dobermans are faithful friends who love their families. They are not vicious attack dogs at all, but they will protect you if they sense danger. Even then, they typically protect their favorite humans by keeping the bad guys cornered, until help arrives. Protecting their family is just one way that they demonstrate their love. They are

20

also accomplished cuddlers, who love belly rubs and ear scratches. Dobermans are highly intelligent and have a great work ethic. They love to be active and mentally stimulated. Dobermans are not very good couch potatoes. They loathe boredom. Instead, they thrive when learning new tasks and working alongside humans, as guard dogs, police dogs, search and rescue dogs, and therapy dogs. If they aren't able to work, they should still be kept active. Long walks, runs, or hikes will help your Doberman stay fit and active.

In many instances, over-breeding has altered the Doberman Pinscher temperament. Irresponsible breeding has produced dogs that are neurotic and prone to chasing their own tails, severe anxiety, and uncontrollable barking. Before adopting a rescue Doberman, you should observe the animal for patterns of neurotic behavior. Even if the dog is not suffering from neurosis, Doberman over-breeding has created dogs that suffer from separation anxiety. When left alone for long periods of time, the anxiety that is evident in chewing, digging, or other destructive behavior.

Are Dobermans Aggressive?

Doberman aggression is a valid concern. After all, this breed of dog often appears on top ten lists of the most dangerous dog breeds. Aggression in Dobermans is, in many cases, an exaggerated stereotype based on misinformation. While it is true that the Doberman breed was developed to be formidable and intimidating while protecting his owner, they were also bred to be obedient and controlled so they would only act aggressively on command. That is a major distinction that should not be overlooked. Most Dobermans today, are no longer working as war dogs or police dogs. Therefore breeders have worked to tone down the aggression. In several studies of various dog breeds, the Doberman Pinscher ranked high in loyalty and playfulness, and low on aggressiveness. Today's Doberman Pinschers are easy going, good-natured animals who are smart, trainable, and loyal…all the hallmarks of a good family dog.

A Doberman will become an important member of your family.

As with all dogs, Doberman Pinschers will be friendlier and more docile if they are socialized as early as possible. While he is still a young pup, you should handle, train, and play with him, so he will learn that humans are kind and trustworthy. The Centers for Disease Control in the United States showed that Dobermans ranked far behind other dog breeds – German Shepherds, Huskies, Rottweilers, Pitt Bulls, Alaskan Malamutes, and dog-wolf hybrids – in animals involved in biting humans. The same study also indicated that the single most important factor in preventing dog bites was the level of responsibility exhibited by the owners of the dog. Dobermans raised to be loving, friendly pets will respond in a loving and friendly way. Dogs raised with violence will respond with violence.

What are the Space Requirements of the Doberman Pinscher?

Dobermans are large dogs that were bred to be hard workers, with energy and endurance to spare. This breed of dog is a top-level athlete. Like all athletes, Dobermans need to stay in great condition, and that means plenty of exercise. Ideally, your home will have a large, fenced-in backyard, so your Doberman is able to run at top speed on a daily basis. If you think your Doberman will get all the exercise he needs by accompanying you on daily walks or jogs, you are wrong. No human can match the stamina of the Doberman; he will not be adequately challenged.

Dobermans can adapt to small houses and apartments if there is adequate outdoor room, and ample opportunities to exercise. If you do have a large outdoor space, your Doberman may not get the amount of rigorous exercise he needs to stay fit and healthy. You need to encourage him to run at high speeds, by playing ball or Frisbee with him. You could even consider having two Dobermans, or another highly-active dog. Two dogs will run together and chase each other, getting a good workout and expending their pent-up energy.

Will a Doberman Pinscher be a Good Addition to My Family?

Absolutely! If the Doberman has been well-trained, adequately socialized, and knows who is boss, he will live up to the "man's best friend" motto. They are true companion dogs and love to interact with their owners. They are extremely intelligent and relish the chance to learn new tricks…and show them off for treats. However, they may not be the best choice for a first dog because they need a strong and capable owner to be the well-established leader of the "pack." Once the Doberman knows his place in the pecking order and has learned to trust and respect the leader, he will happily accept his position in the family and show devotion to all the family members. An inexperienced dog owner may not be able to provide the consistency needed to curb the Doberman's stubbornness.

Will a Doberman Pinscher Get Along with my Children?

Generally speaking, yes. Dobermans are great with kids. However, all interactions between children and dogs should be supervised. That goes for all breeds of dogs, not just Doberman Pinschers. Also, children need to be taught at an early age how to behave around dogs and how to treat dogs. Most often, when a dog nips at a child, it is because the child has pulled the animal's tail or ear or tried to climb on his back and ride him like a pony. Explaining to all young children that this is unacceptable behavior, goes a long way in making sure the dog and child relationship remains positive.

Dobermans instinctively know they should protect their family.

Dobermans tend to be very protective of children and seem to intuitively know that youngsters are more vulnerable. The Doberman's guard dog characteristics mean that he will keep an alert eye on children in order to protect them from harm. Sometimes, he is too protective though. If a stranger is near the child and does something sudden and unexpected, like moving quickly, raising his hands, or making a loud noise, the Doberman may maneuver himself between the stranger and the child, issuing a warning to the stranger in the form of a growl. He will back down, though, once his trusted pack leader/owner commands it.

Overall, a well-raised Doberman is tolerant and gentle with children.

Will a Doberman Get Along with my Other Pets?

Doberman Pinschers are easy-going, genial dogs that will, most likely, get along just fine with other dogs in your household. There are a few things to keep in mind, however. First, male Dobermans are more prone to same sex aggression than some other breeds of dogs, so two male dogs living together may create friction. The Doberman Pinscher has a dominant personality and will attempt to be the "top dog." If he is in a household with another male dog, the two animals will jockey for the position of dominance. If you want to keep multiple dogs, consider a male-female combination (spayed and neutered, of course), or two females.

Dobermans are powerful and athletic and, therefore, they like to play hard. They will expect the other dogs living with them to keep up. If you have a less active dog, you may notice that your Doberman will try to goad him into playing.

As a breed, Dobermans have a high prey drive and will instinctively chase a small animal that runs away from him, such as a rabbit or cat. It may take strong and consistent training to stop your Doberman Pinscher from chasing your poor kitty. If they are properly introduced to other dogs and to cats, and well-trained to heed the commands of his owner, Dobermans quickly learn to co-habitat with other pets. You may even find you Doberman cuddled up napping with your cat or frolicking with your other dog.

Will a Doberman Pinscher Require a Lot of Attention?

Dobermans are natural athletes.

There are two characteristics of the Doberman dog breed that factor into their attention requirements…their intelligence and their love of human companionship.

Because Dobermans are one of the smartest breeds of dog, they need constant mental stimulation, along with physical stimulation. If you think your Doberman Pinscher will be content chained to a doghouse or staying in a crate all day, you will soon find out how wrong you are. A bored Doberman will find things to keep his active mind satisfied, and you might not like what he chooses. Instead of sitting by and watching him destroy your couch, you will need to give your Doberman plenty of attention and toys that will keep his attention.

Second, Dobermans love people. They long to be devoted companions and want nothing more than to be by the side of their owner. The Doberman was designed to work alongside humans and, even when they are not working, they are still happiest when they are sitting next to their favorite humans. Dobermans require a lot of daily exercise, and it is possible to combine their workout with companion time, by playing ball or Frisbee with them, or taking them for a long run.

What are the Grooming Requirements of the Doberman Pinscher?

Dobermans are fairly low maintenance dogs. Their short fur is easy to care for…you can get away with a quick brushing just once a week. They shed only moderately, and brushing will help loosen the dead hair. Dobermans don't need to be bathed often. In fact, you can simply wipe them down with a damp towel most of the time. When they do need a bath, you can wash them with dog shampoo, and let them shake dry. They will need to have their toenails trimmed regularly, and their teeth brushed, but other than that, grooming a Doberman is a snap.

CHAPTER 4

What Are the Breed Standards for the Doberman Pinscher?

When the Doberman Pinscher was developed in Germany, it is believed several different breeds of dogs were used to create this powerful and protective dog. The result is a unique breed, unlike other dogs. The breed standards for the Doberman Pinscher reflect this. Strong, muscular, and powerful, the Doberman Pinscher is easily identified by his distinctive silhouette.

How Big Do Dobermans Get?

Full grown Dobermans are strong and sturdy animals. Dobermans are a medium sized dog, but a well-built and muscular one. Male Dobermans can stand 26 to 28 inches (66.04 to 71.12 centimeters) in height, while female Dobermans are slightly shorter at 24 to 26 inches (60.96 to 66.04 centimeters). They are sturdy and robust; therefore, the males can weigh between 75 and 100 pounds (34.01 and 45.36 kilograms), and the females can reach between 60 and 90 pounds (27.21 and 40.82 kilograms).

What are the Breed Standards for Dobermans?

A healthy, fit adult Doberman should be squarely built and muscular with a long head and almond-shaped eyes. The dog's chest is broad and chiseled, giving the Doberman a stately and elegant silhouette. In some countries, including the United States, the ears of the Doberman are cropped, so they stand erect. The tails are also docked when the animal is a young pup. In many countries, however, the practice of cropping ears and docking tails is falling out of favor, and breeders are opting for a more natural look. In fact, ear cropping, and tail docking is illegal in many countries.

The Doberman is a powerful, muscular dog.

Today's Dobermans are sleeker and trimmer than their ancestors, as breeders have altered the original appearance of the Doberman Pinscher. The dog's temperament has also been toned down over the years, as the animal transitioned from a fierce guard dog to a playful family pet.

What is the Doberman's Personality?

Doberman Pinschers are highly intelligent, extremely athletic, and abundantly active. They are also playful, loyal, and protective. Dobermans are classified as working dogs and, indeed, the animals are well-suited for hard work. They exhibit impressive endurance and strength, making them ideal for military and police work. But they are also sensitive and people-oriented, so they are also used as therapy dogs and for search-and-rescue work. The Doberman's quick and eager brain wants to be stimulated and challenged. This is not a dog breed that is content to be on the couch all day. Rather, he needs to keep both his mind and his muscles working. This can sometimes pose a problem for busy families. Dobermans are wonderful companion dogs, so you can solve this dilemma by including your Doberman on family adventures, such as trips to the park and afternoons at the beach.

What are the Accepted Coat Colors for Doberman Pinschers?

Traditionally, Dobermans are known as black dogs with brown accents. However, there are actually five accepted coat colors for Doberman Pinschers. Dobermans can be born with black, red, blue, white, or fawn colored coats.

What Should I Know About Black Dobermans?

The smooth, sleek dogs that we have come to identify with the Doberman Pinscher is predominantly black with brownish, or rust colored, fur on his ears, eyebrows, cheeks, and the interior of his legs. Every so often, however, a Doberman puppy is born all black, lacking the brown accents on his coat. All black Dobermans, also called melanistic Dobermans, are not included in the accepted breed standards for the dog, and although the all-black Doberman puppy may make an excellent pet, these animals should not be bred. Responsible Doberman breeders care about the breed as a whole and will take steps to ensure a healthy bloodline, free of mutations like the melanistic all-black Doberman.

Red Dobermans are tan or light brown in color.

What Should I Know About Red Dobermans?

Although they are called red Dobermans in many parts of the world, the fur of these dogs is light brown, with reddish tints. Red Dobermans are also called brown Dobermans or chocolate Dobermans. The shades of red can range from a brassy copper to a deep mocha. The red Doberman is actually two-tones, with lighter shades of red or brown on his face, ears, eyebrows, and legs.

What Should I Know About Blue Dobermans?

Blue Dobermans are not as wide-spread as black and red Dobermans. The blue fur color is actually a dilution of the traditional black fur, which results in a coat that is silvery, gray, or purplish in color. Because of this, the blue Doberman is often called the gray Doberman. Many breeders shy away from breeding blue Dobermans, and these dogs are sometimes disqualified from competing in dog shows. The color variance, however, is not viewed as a result of irresponsible breeding. Therefore the dogs are not deemed inferior or flawed. They can still make wonderful family pets.

What Should I Know About Fawn Dobermans?

Like the blue Doberman, the Fawn Doberman gets its unique coat color from a dilution of the brownish fur of the red Doberman. Also called Isabella Dobermans, the fawn Doberman can be the product of good breeding practices. Even though they may be eliminated from participating in dog shows, fawn Dobermans are genetically sound if they are the product of good, responsible breeding.

What Should I Know About White Dobermans?

White Dobermans are not included in the accepted breed standards. Many people assume the white Dobermans are albinos, they are not true albinos, although they do exhibit some characteristics of albino animals, such as poor eyesight. The white Dobermans may look exotic and interesting, but they are a result of irresponsible inbreeding. They are prone to health and behavioral issues. The dog may get easily confused or feel threatened because it cannot fully see its surroundings and lash out by biting. Several countries have banned the breeding of white Dobermans because of the instability of their temperament, and because it is regarded as cruel and inhumane to continue to breed mutated dogs.

CHAPTER 5

Where Do I Find Doberman Pinscher Puppies?

ongratulations! You have decided that a Doberman Pinscher is the perfect dog for you and your family. The next step is finding one. The popularity of Dobermans mean that you should have no difficulty finding a Doberman Pinscher breeder near you, but it also means that you will need to wade through the choices to weed out puppy mill breeders and naïve backyard breeders to find a reputable breeder that produces top-quality Doberman puppies. Here are some suggestions for evaluating the Doberman breeders your meet and selecting the best puppy for you and your family.

How Do I Find a Responsible Doberman Pinscher Breeder?

A quick Google search will show you plenty of Doberman puppies for sale near you, but before you purchase the first puppy you see, you should evaluate the quality of the breeder. To do this, you should have an understanding of how responsible breeders run their facilities, red flags that indicate the operation is a puppy mill, and questions you should ask the breeder.

What Should I Ask a Doberman Breeder During a Phone Interview?

Start with a list of questions that you want to ask a breeder. A responsible breeder will not make you feel stupid for asking questions. On the contrary, they welcome your questions. They want to make sure they are placing their puppies with responsible pet owners, and your questions are an indication that you care. In fact, the responsible breeder will also ask you several questions. Again, they want to make sure their puppy is a good fit for your family and your lifestyle. If the breeder makes you feel uncomfortable about asking questions, it may be that they are trying to hide something.

To help you narrow down the choices of Doberman breeders, you should call them and ask some of your questions over the phone. You will gain much better insight by talking directly to the breeder, and not relying on texting or emailing. And you will be more focused on the questions and answers when you are talking to the breeder over the phone instead of at the kennel, where you may be distracted by the adorable puppies. Start by asking some basic questions, such as how long they have been breeding Dobermans and why they chose this breed of dog. You can also ask if the puppy's parents are on site and available for you to meet. A responsible breeder will want you to meet the parents. Also ask about veterinarian visits, de-worming, vaccinations, and general health. All of these questions should be easily answered by a competent breeder.

What Should I Look For, When I Visit a Doberman Pinscher Breeder's Kennel?

Use the information gleaned from your telephone interviews to narrow the options down to two or three breeders. Then you can schedule a visit to the breeder's kennels. Use these visits to further evaluate the cleanliness and quality of the facility. Observe the dogs and see if they look healthy, well-fed, and well-cared for. Observe where the dogs are housed to see how many litters of pups there are and if there are other animals, like chickens or goats, housed in the same building. Observe how the puppies interact with the breeder and with each other to see if they are playful, friendly, and socialized. Pick up a few of the puppies yourself to see how they behave for you and to see if they are used to being held. When you hold them, look in their eyes to see if they are clear, alert, and bright. You could also sit down on the floor and let the puppies come to you. You may want to avoid picking the alpha puppy as he may be aggressive and too much of a bully. But you should also avoid the shy, timid puppy that is too scared to come to you.

Before you visit the kennel, you should mentally prepare yourself to walk away if you are not happy with the condition that you observe, or you are not satisfied with the answers the breeder gives to your questions. Be wary if the breeder seems to be giving you the hard sell or pushing you to pick out a puppy quickly. A responsible breeder wants you to take your time to get to know each puppy before you make your decision. It is easy to be so captivated by the overabundance of puppy cuteness that you make decisions with your heart and not your head, but you should walk away if you see any red flags.

Responsible Doberman breeders strive to produce top-quality, healthy puppies.

You might not be able to bring your Doberman puppy home that day anyway. Responsible Doberman Pinscher breeders will not release a puppy to his new home until he is seven or eight weeks old, completely weaned, fully vaccinated, and has been socialized. Once you decide on a puppy, the responsible breeder will ask you to read and sign a breeder's contract that provides you with some guarantee about the health of the animal. The breeder will also give you documentation of the Doberman puppy's medical and vaccination history, pedigree, diet, and the purebred registration application.

CHAPTER 6

What Should I Know About Doberman Pinschers and Puppy Mills?

Y ou should know that there are plenty of responsible Doberman Pinscher breeders who are concerned about upholding the standards of the breed and producing top quality puppies. But you should also know that there are plenty of Doberman Pinscher breeders who are only in the business to make money. The quality of the dogs they produce is of secondary concern. When it comes time for you to shop around for a Doberman puppy to call your own, you should take care to make sure you are dealing with a reputable breeder and not a puppy mill.

Are Backyard Breeders the Same as Puppy Mill Breeders?

There is, however, a step between puppy mills and responsible breeders. Those are the backyard breeders. A backyard breeder is a person who owns a few Dobermans as pets, then decides to breed one of them with another one of their dogs or with a friend's

Doberman. They may plan to keep one or two of the Doberman puppies, but they will sell the rest. As amateur dog breeders, the backyard breeder may take impeccable care of their dogs and have a great love for the Doberman breed, but they may not be as knowledgeable about breed standards, responsible breeding practices, and how to breed for temperament or specific physical qualities. The dogs they produce are probably healthy and happy and will make great pets, but they may also have some underlying genetic problems.

A great Doberman begins with the breeder.

What Sets a Responsible Doberman Pinscher Breeder Apart from a Puppy Mill Breeder?

A well-established, responsible Doberman Pinscher breeder is dedicated to breeding high-quality, healthy dogs. They typically have years of experience breeding Dobermans and understand accepted breeding practices. Most often, they are dedicated to just one or two breeds of dog. Their kennels are clean and free of hazards. Their dogs are regularly seen by a veterinarian, are properly socialized, and are in good health.

On the other hand, puppy mills are breeding operations in which the kennel owners put profits ahead of the welfare of the puppies. To maximize profits, puppy mill owners will sell puppies that are younger than eight weeks old, sell unvaccinated puppies, and breed the females as soon as possible without giving them adequate time to recover from the previous litter of puppies. Many times, the dogs are kept in dirty, overcrowded conditions. They receive little to no socialization and are not taken to a veterinarian for a puppy check-up. They may be fed inferior food because it is cheaper in cost and fed lesser amounts than recommended.

What are the Risks Associated with Puppy Mill Dogs?

Doberman Pinschers that come from puppy mills are prone to genetic issues, congenital problems, and other health abnormalities, including epilepsy, respiratory diseases, and skeletal defects. This is because the puppy mill breeders are primarily focused on the profits that can be made from selling cute puppies, not on producing top-notch Doberman Pinschers.

Puppy mills stay in business because there are plenty of naïve, unsuspecting people who, when they are looking for a puppy, simply answer newspaper or internet ads for Doberman puppies for sale and don't know what they should look for in a reputable breeder and kennel. There are, however, some red flags that you should look out for. First, if a breeder that you call suggests that you meet somewhere other than at their kennel, you should be suspicious. A responsible Doberman Pinscher breeder would welcome you to their kennel. In fact, they wish you would come. They want you to see your puppy's parents and see how your puppy interacts with his littermates. They want you to see for yourself how well-cared-for the dogs are and how clean the kennel is. In short, reputable breeders welcome transparency. Puppy mill breeders, on the other hand, don't want you to see the crowded cages and unsanitary living conditions. They want to hide the fact that there are multiple litters of puppies at their kennel, and that there are diseases and parasites.

Are Pet Stores the Same as Puppy Mills?

You may be tempted to buy your Doberman Pinscher puppy from the pet store at your local mall, but you should question where the pet store gets their puppies. Most pet stores get their puppies from puppy mills. In fact, the Humane Society of the United States estimates that 99% of the puppies sold at pet stores were born at a puppy mill, despite what the employee of the pet store has been trained to tell you. Further investigations conducted by the Humane Society have uncovered the fact that some breeders who routinely sell to pet stores are guilty of repeated violations of the Federal Animal Welfare Act. Responsible Doberman Pinscher breeders won't sell their puppies to a pet store to be sold. This is a violation of the code of ethics of nearly every dog breed club. But responsible breeders are also concerned about the futures of their Doberman puppies. They want to meet the owners, so they can assure themselves that the puppy is going to a good home with people who will love him and take proper care of him.

What are the Warning Signs of a Puppy Mill Breeder?

When you begin looking for a new Doberman puppy to join your family, be on the lookout for some warning signs that you may be dealing with a puppy mill owner. If the owner tries to sell you a puppy that is younger than eight weeks, it may be because he is just trying to move out his merchandise as quickly as possible. Also, if the Doberman Pinscher pup isn't vaccinated and has not yet seen a veterinarian, it may be a sign that the breeder is trying to cut costs by foregoing routine medical visits. When you meet the puppy, observe to see if he is clean, active, and playful. If he seems shy, quiet, and reserved, those are signs that he had not been socialized or has endured some stress or trauma. Lastly, ask about the dog's pedigree and lineage. A reputable dog breeder will be able to give you a pedigree showing the lineage and health history several generations back, typically three to five generations. A puppy mill breeder may not want to be forthcoming with this information, because it may show inbreeding.

Buying a puppy can be an emotional experience, but you should make decisions with your brain, and not your heart. If you suspect you are dealing with a puppy mill operator, you should walk away, no matter how cute the little Doberman puppy may be or how compelled you feel to "save" the puppy from his puppy mill surroundings. If you do business with a puppy mill, you are supporting this type of business and contributing to its continuation. If every puppy buyer refused to purchase from a puppy mill facility, the practice would eventually die out. You will also be helping the Doberman breed as a whole because the responsible breeders act as caretakers of the dog breed, ensuring genetic quality and overall health.

CHAPTER 7

How Do I Prepare to Bring My Doberman Pinscher Home?

The more you prepare to bring your new Doberman Pinscher puppy home, the smoother the transition will be. Well before you bring your new little bundle of love home, you need to make sure that you, your family, and your house are all ready to welcome your furry new best friend. Your goal is to make your Doberman puppy's transition as stress-free as possible, so he is happy and well-adjusted in his new home. This chapter discusses the puppy supplies that you need to have on hand before you welcome home your new Doberman Pinscher puppy, as well as the steps you need to take to safely puppy-proof your home.

How Do I Puppy Proof My Home for My Doberman Pinscher Puppy?

As you await the day that you can bring your new Doberman puppy home and make him part of your family, you can make ready your house by puppy-proofing it. Your Doberman puppy's safety and well-being should be your top priority, which means you need to take the time to rid your home of anything that will present a

45

danger to him. Remember that your puppy's point of view is much different than yours. Crawl on your hands and knees will help you see things through your puppy's eyes. You will notice potential hazards that you may not have noticed before, such as electrical cords or tiny objects left under furniture. These can become dangerous if the puppy finds them and chews on them.

Go room by room to puppy-proof your house. In the bathroom, make sure that cleaning supplies, such as toilet bowl cleaners and shower cleaners, are kept safely out of reach. Remind everyone in your family to get in the habit of putting the toilet seat down. Your puppy may try to drink the toilet bowl water if he gets thirsty…or if he's just curious. The cleaning chemicals in the toilet water – and other things that may happen to be in there – could be hazardous to your dog. You may want to consider getting a bathroom trash can with a lid and encouraging your family to be diligent about throwing away bathroom items that can be a choking hazard for a curious puppy, such as cotton swabs, rubber hair ties, disposable razors, bottle caps, and toilet paper.

An inquisitive Doberman puppy might be able to nose open kitchen cupboards and get into boxes or bags of food. He may even be able to open the cupboard under the kitchen sink where you most likely store your dishwashing soap, floor cleaner, and other cleaning supplies. If your cupboard doors don't close securely, you may wish to install child safety latches on them, for the safety of your Doberman.

Like all dogs, Dobermans have an acute sense of smell. They enjoy things that smell like you and will respond by chewing on them. This included the clothes you leave discarded on your bedroom floor...socks, underwear, belts, shoes and more. You should get in the habit of putting your dirty laundry in a hamper with a lid, and not in a pile on the floor. And then there are the more expensive items that our playful Doberman may find, chew, and destroy...such as jewelry, watches, eyeglasses, and hearing aids. If you leave these items on your nightstand, you may be inadvertently tempting your new puppy.

In other parts of your home, attempt to move all power cords, extension cords, cell phone and laptop chargers, and earbuds, so they are out of reach for a curious puppy. If there are cords that you cannot remove or hide, you can keep them out of reach of your Doberman puppy by running them through PVC piping. Just as you would do if you were baby proofing a house for a toddler, remove things from the floor, coffee tables, couches, and end tables. Doberman puppies like to chew on throw pillows, magazines, shoes, children's toys, and afghans. Puppies may not be able to negotiate stairs at first. A baby gate placed securely across the staircase will help to keep your Doberman puppy from taking a tumble until he grows more confident with steps.

The garage can hold a number tempting hazards for a curious little Doberman puppy. Cleaning, pest control, lawn and garden, and automotive chemicals can be toxic and potentially deadly. Tools, garden equipment, and sporting equipment can be a choking hazard.

How Do I Introduce My Doberman Puppy to My Family and Other Pets?

You may be envisioning the moment you bring you Doberman puppy home and are picturing a happy moment in which everyone – your family members, your other pets, and your new puppy – all become best friends. Chances are things won't go as smoothly as you imagine. In reality, your little Doberman puppy may be anxious, stressed, and overwhelmed. Your family, especially young children, may be overbearing. And your other pets may react aggressively or become territorial. There are steps you can take, however, to make your puppy's homecoming a happier experience for all. The key is to be properly prepared.

Purchase your supplies before you bring your pup home.

Are your other pets used to being around other dogs? If not, you may want to get them accustomed to interacting with other animals before you bring your puppy home. Take them to a dog park or visit friends with pets, so they learn how to behave properly with other pets. You may want to let your older dog meet your new puppy for the first time in a neutral location, such as the park. This will reduce the chances that your older dog will get territorial and possessive. If you are still unsure how the animals will act together, you may want to have baby gates on hand, so you can keep them separated if you feel that is necessary.

Talk to your family members, especially younger children, about how they should act on homecoming day. They should refrain from screaming, squealing, and running around so that you can reduce the noise and chaos in your home. You should strive to create a calming environment, so your new puppy associates his new home with peace and love, not pandemonium. It might be hard for youngsters to remember this once they see the adorable little puppy… you may have to gently remind them to keep their voices down and to avoid roughhousing. You may be excited about your puppy's arrival and want to show him off to your friends and extended family members, but that can wait. Homecoming day should be low-key and a time to let your puppy get acquainted with his new family and new surroundings.

What Doberman Pinscher Supplies Do I Need?

There are some supplies you will need to have on hand for your new Doberman puppy. We suggest that you have everything you need on hand before you bring your puppy home, so you don't have to interrupt homecoming day by zipping out to the store to get supplies. This will give you more time to bond with your Doberman. So what Doberman supplies do you need?

You will need dishes for food and water. These are available at any pet store. You can select individual plastic or stainless-steel bowls, or a single dish that has two bowls built in. A playful Doberman puppy may gnaw on a plastic dish, so you may want to invest in the stainless-steel ones. As for the single or double bowl dishes, it just comes down to personal preference. Some people like the single bowl ones so they can fill up the water without accidentally spilling the dog food, and vice versa. Whichever one you pick, you should find a spill proof design. A Doberman puppy can get excited and spill over his dishes in his exuberance. You may find yourself constantly mopping up messes and refilling the bowls. An automatic waterer, that continuously fills your dog's water bowl, is a good solution. Automatic feeders are also available, but these make it more difficult to monitor how much food your puppy is getting.

You should also have puppy food and treats on hand. Ask your Doberman breeder what kind of food they have been giving your Doberman puppy and buy some of that brand. If you would rather feed him a different brand of food, that's okay. You can slowly switch foods after your puppy has acclimated to his new home. You don't want to hit him with too many changes at once…it may increase his anxiety levels and cause digestive issues. You should also ask the breeder for a jug or two of the water your puppy is used to drinking. Different tap water has different tastes, and your puppy may refuse to drink unfamiliar water. He will eventually get used to your water, but you don't want to have too many changes at once. You can have some treats ready to give your puppy but be careful that you don't overload him with too many treats, just because he is so cute that you want to spoil him. He may develop an upset tummy.

You should have a collar or harness, and a leash on hand before you bring your puppy home. The collar should be made of a soft material, like nylon or leather, that won't rub and chafe. The collar should fit loosely, but not too loosely. A good rule of thumb is to find a collar that allows you to easily slip two fingers under it. If you can, the collar fits well, but if you can't, the collar is too snug. The collar should really be used just to hold identification tags with your contact information in case your Doberman runs away and becomes lost. When you take your Doberman for walks, you should attach the leash to a harness instead of his collar. The harness goes across the dog's chest and is safer than a collar. A rambunctious puppy will run and pull against the leash and may injure his neck. The harness should also be smooth and soft, so it doesn't cause sores. As for the leash, you can buy leather, nylon, or chain leashes. Any of these will work well, but a curious puppy may chew on a leather or nylon leash, compromising its integrity.

You should have a dog crate and a comfy doggie bed ready for your new Doberman puppy. After all, he is still a baby and will need plenty of sleep. The crate will soon become your puppy's safe zone, a place where he feels secure and comfortable. It is a place where he can go if he is feeling overwhelmed or tired. It should be as comfortable as possible. A plush, thick doggie bed with bumper sides will give him an enclosed, secure feeling. If the doggie bed is too large for him, he may not feel as secure. You should purchase a doggie bed that is easily washed so you can clean it often, yet durable so your Doberman won't tear it apart with his chewing.

You should also have a few Doberman toys available for your puppy to play with. Although you will not find specific Doberman Pinscher dog toys, you can purchase high-quality, durable puppy toys for medium sized dogs. Pick designs that can't be easily ripped apart and without small pieces that can cause a choking hazard. Doberman puppies like tug-o-war-type toys because they help build strength, but they also like balls and Frisbees. You don't need to shower your puppy with an overabundance of toys, but he should have enough to keep him occupied. Remember, if he becomes bored, he may chew on household objects, like your slippers or couch cushions or table legs.

Dobermans require very little grooming, but you may want to have some gentle puppy shampoo at your house. An excited little fella may roll in the mud when he is playing outdoors and needs a quick bath. Look for shampoos that are mild and chemical free, so they don't irritate his tender puppy skin. You can purchase a dog brush, but the Doberman's short coat doesn't require daily brushing.

CHAPTER 8

What Should I Feed My Doberman Pinscher?

Your Doberman Pinscher is an elite athlete, and he needs the proper fuel to power his magnificent body. But it may be difficult to know what dog food product to feed your Doberman to keep him fit and healthy when you see the vast array of dog foods that fill the pet store shelves. In this chapter, we will discuss the nutritional requirements of the Doberman Pinscher, as well as the differences between canned and dry dog food, and foods that can be harmful to your dog.

What Should I Feed My Adult Doberman Pinscher?

The powerful and active Doberman Pinscher needs a high-quality diet that is also easy to digest. When selecting the dog food that you will be feeding your Doberman, always carefully read the labels on the packages. The first ingredient listed on the label should be meat, either beef, lamb, or chicken. After meat, the next ingredients should be whole grains, such as brown rice, and vegetables, including sweet potatoes. Avoid dog foods that list animal byproducts as the first ingredient, as well as ones that list cereal grains like corn and wheat, or fillers that add bulk to the food. The dog food should also contain fatty acids, such as flaxseed or safflower oils, to help keep the Doberman's coat shiny and healthy.

If your Doberman is very active and gets regular exercise, you may need a higher calorie intake than a dog that is less active. Follow the dog food manufacture's requirements on the dog food package as to how much to feed your dog but adjust the amount up or down based on your individual dog's activity level. Divide the daily food quantity into two to four separate meals, so your Doberman has time to digest one meal before it is time for the next one. If you think your Doberman is underweight or overweight, you should check with your veterinarian to discuss a feeding schedule.

What Should I Feed My Doberman Pinscher Puppy?

Doberman puppies have different nutritional needs than full-grown Doberman Pinschers. That's why they should be fed a dog food formulated for growing puppies. If you try feeding your Doberman puppy adult dog food, he will not receive the protein, calories, fat, and minerals that he needs to grow strong and healthy. Doberman puppies between the ages of 6 and 12 weeks should be fed four times a day. Allow the puppy to eat his fill for about ten minutes, and then remove the food dish. Dispose of the unused food. You should carefully watch as your puppy eats and increase the amount of food as he gets older.

Once your Doberman puppy reaches 3 months of age, you can start decreasing the number of meals from 4 to 3. Between the ages of 3 and 6 months, your Doberman puppy will start to lose its puppy pudge, and start to acquire the slim, trim physique of an adult dog. After his first birthday, you can switch from the high-protein puppy food to an adult food.

What Should I Feed My Aging Doberman Pinscher?

Doberman Pinschers begin slowing down and feeling their age when they are about 7 or 8 years old. They become less active, therefore their caloric intake and nutritional requirements change. If they continue to eat their adult maintenance diet, they will put on weight. When your dog starts to show signs of age, switch from an adult formula dog food to one specifically designed for senior dogs. Maintaining proper nutrition will help your Doberman avert age-related problems and illnesses. But not all senior dog food is the same. Some have a higher calorie count than others, so it is important to read the labels on commercial dog foods and to discuss nutritional changes with your veterinarian.

What are the Nutritional Requirements of the Doberman Pinscher?

Dobermans need a high-protein diet to keep their muscular bodies properly fueled. At a minimum, they should be consuming a diet that is 25% protein. Active and working Dobermans should have a little more protein in their food, but you must be careful. Too much protein can lead to kidney problems. It is important to know, however, that not all proteins are the same. Look for foods that list beef, chicken, and lamb as a protein source, not animal by products.

Dobermans also need complex carbohydrates in their diet. Complex carbohydrates burn slowly, so the dog's blood sugar stays consistent. Carbohydrates can come from a variety of sources, and some are better than others. Sweet potatoes are a great slow-burning carb, as are whole grains such as brown rice.

An average sized, adult Doberman Pinscher should consume about 1850 calories per day. If the dog is extremely active or a working dog, the number of calories should increase to about 2220 calories per day. Older and less active Dobermans need only about 1335 daily calories.

What is the Link Between Nutrition and Health Issues in Doberman Pinschers?

Food provides the building blocks for a healthy dog. If a dog is fed inferior food, he will not be able to reach peak health and fitness. Dobermans demand a high-quality diet, more so than other dog breeds. By ensuring that your Doberman Pinscher is eating the best food for his breed, size, age, and lifestyle, you will help to reduce the chances of disease.

For example, Dobermans can be prone to low blood sugar, or hypoglycemia. If they have a diet that is rich in simple, quick-burning carbohydrates, they will experience blood sugar spikes and crashes throughout the day. But if they have slower burning, complex carbohydrates in their diet, their blood sugar remains at a constant level throughout the day.

Kidney disease can also be a problem for Dobermans, and a diet that is too rich in protein can aggravate the problem. You should consult your veterinarian regarding the proper amount of protein your individual dog should have in his diet.

Hypothyroidism is another condition that is commonly found in Dobermans. With this condition, the dog's thyroid does not produce enough T3 and T4 hormones, causing the animal to gain weight, despite exercise and diet restrictions. To control the effects of hypothyroidism, your dog should eat high-quality, whole foods that include meats, vegetables, roots, and fruits, while avoiding processed grains and fillers that are common in cheaper commercial dog foods.

Bloat is a common problem in dogs, like the Doberman, that have deep chests and narrow waists. Bloat happens when the dog's stomach fills with gas, causing it to twist. Bloat is a life-threatening condition and requires an emergency visit to the veterinarian. To avoid bloat, feed your dog several smaller meals throughout the day so his body can digest them more easily. Adding a little water to his dog food will also help reduce gas build up. You should also avoid strenuous exercise right after meal time.

Should I Feed My Doberman Pinscher Dry Dog Food or Canned Dog Food?

When shopping for food for your Doberman Pinscher, you will quickly notice that commercial dog food is available in either dry form, called kibbles, or wet form, in cans. You may even ask yourself, "which one is best?" but that is not an easy question to answer. There are pros and cons to both types of dog food and understanding them can help you make an informed decision about what is best for your dog.

Doberman canned food, because of the high moisture content, may help to reduce gas build-up in the dog's stomach that can lead to bloat. Canned food is generally tastier with a stronger odor, so finicky dogs may prefer it. If you have an older Doberman or one who is ill or missing teeth, the softer canned food may be easier to chew, and therefore the dog will eat a full meal. Canned dog food, however, is more prone to spoilage and waste. Also, the cans are a predetermined size so you may need multiple cans to feed a dog as large as a Doberman. Also, ass a general rule, canned dog food is more costly than dry dog food.

Doberman dry dog food is easier to measure out and easier to store. It is more convenient when you and your Doberman are out and about for the day, and the smell won't offend others. Kibbles can be left out for longer periods of time without fear of spoilage. Kibbles are also less expensive.

It is important to remember that dog food ranges in quality within dry and canned varieties. You can find very good and very poor-quality foods in each type. Therefore the decision whether to feed your Doberman Pinscher kibbles or canned really comes down to personal preferences. Whichever one you choose, you should remain consistent. If you switch back and forth between canned and kibbles, you will disrupt your Doberman's digestive system.

Should I Consider Feeding My Doberman Pinscher a Homemade Diet?

Making homemade dog food for you Doberman may give you more control over what your dog is eating, but it is a big commitment to make. Not only does it require time and effort, but the cost can be quite high. Before you make the commitment, you should know what you are getting yourself into. Do your research. Learn about the nutritional requirements of the Doberman and then find a homemade dog food recipe that you feel satisfies these requirements. Do a few trial batches so that you get a realistic idea of how much time, effort, and money it takes to produce.

Prior to solidifying your commitment to making your own dog food, consider this. The commercial dog food that is on the market today has been developed by animal nutritionists, scientists, biologists, and veterinarians after hours and hours of exhaustive trial and error research. It may not be possible for you to replicate that research and by simply looking up recipes on the internet.

You should also discuss your plans to make your Doberman homemade dog food with your veterinarian and get his or her feedback. He or she may be able to give you pointers or suggest a specific recipe. But making your veterinarian aware of your diet plans for your dog is a good preventative step. That way your veterinarian can be on the look-out for potential diet-related problems or issues at your dog's check-ups.

When you start the process of making your own dog food, you will need to start with a good recipe. Like commercial dog foods, not all homemade dog food recipes are the same. You will need to start with a good source of protein, such as animal meat or eggs, and add to that carbohydrates from vegetables and grains, and a source of calcium and fats. You should follow the recipe exactly and not substitute any ingredients. Consider purchasing a food scale so you can make sure that you are adding the correct amount of ingredients to the mix. Also, make sure you are thoroughly cooking the meat to kill lingering bacteria. The dog food is meant to keep your Doberman in tip-top shape, so you will need to ensure that you are giving him a safe product.

What Should I Know About Giving My Doberman Pinscher Dog Treats?

Treats are a great reward when training your Doberman Pinscher. He will learn faster with positive reinforcement, and a tasty treat fits the bill. You may be tempted to spoil your Doberman with a few extra treats for being such a good boy but try to control how many treats he gets. Too much of a good thing can be bad news for your Doberman's digestive system. They can also spoil his appetite, so he won't eat his dinner. Treats provide empty calories and don't enhance his overall health. In fact, some treats are made with fillers and artificial ingredients that, while tasty, should be avoided. Be sure the read the ingredients listed on the label of the dog treats, just like you do with the dog food packages. You could also offer homemade treats on an occasional basis. Peanut butter, pumpkin, cooked sweet potatoes, and green beans are good choices.

What Food Should My Doberman Pinscher Avoid?

Just because you love a specific food doesn't mean your Doberman should eat it too. In fact, many foods that are just fine for human consumption can make your Doberman Pinscher extremely sick. You should avoid giving your dog table scraps and any human food at all unless you are absolutely certain it is safe for him to eat. And, then, only give it to him in small portions. Some nuts, like walnuts and Macadamia nuts, can make your dog ill. Onions, garlic, and chives can cause the red blood cells to decrease. Dark chocolate can affect the dog's nervous system and cause seizures. Grapes and raisins can be toxic and lead to liver damage and kidney failure. Avocados can cause diarrhea. Peach and plum pits release a substance akin to cyanide when they are digested. Coffee, tea, and alcoholic beverages can also be detrimental to your Doberman's well-being.

Despite what the cartoons tell us, dogs should not be given bones to chew on. The bones can splinter apart and lodge in the Doberman's throat or intestinal tract. This will lead to tissue damage and blockage, which may require surgery.

Can I Feed My Doberman Pinscher a Gluten-Free or Vegan Diet?

People are finding that eating wheat products or animal-based products either negatively impact their overall health or go against their deeply held personal beliefs, therefore we are seeing more and more people adopting gluten-free or vegan diets for themselves and their families. Dogs are also a part of the family, so can you feed your Doberman Pinscher a vegan or gluten-free diet?

Dobermans love fruits and vegetables.

First, let us review the evolutionary biology of the domesticated dog. Dogs evolved from wolves thousands of years ago and, at the time, both species were strictly meat-eaters. Wolves have remained true carnivores, but domesticated dogs have adapted over time, so now they are able to eat starchy foods and to extract some of their nutrients from plant sources. Domesticated dogs no longer need a diet of one hundred percent meat. Although they will eat grains and vegetables, they retain their original desire for meat. If you offer your Doberman a bowl of meat and a bowl of vegetables, he will choose the meat. It is just in his biological make-up.

Remember that Dobermans are athletic, active animals and you need to properly fuel their muscular bodies. You should discuss your desire to feed your Doberman a vegan or vegetarian diet with your veterinarian or pet nutritionist and seek their advice and feedback. He or she will be able to help you select the right plant-based foods to meet your dog's nutritional needs. Your dog's digestive system is different than yours and, therefore, the plant-based foods that satisfy your needs may not be good enough for your Doberman. By working closely with your veterinarian or pet nutritionist, you may be able to devise a vegan diet for your dog that will respect your ethical concerns while providing him with the necessary nutrients.

Gluten, a wheat enzyme, can cause digestive problems and allergic reactions in both humans and dogs. Often, if a dog has a skin disorder that cannot be attributed to another cause, it may be from eating wheat gluten. Luckily, many dog food manufacturers recognize the dangers that occur from gluten and, as awareness of gluten sensitivities has increased, are developing commercial dog food products that are gluten-free. They are using cereal grains, such as brown rice, in place of wheat in their products. Reading the ingredients on the dog food packaging will alert you to the addition of wheat products in the food so you can avoid buying it for your dog.

CHAPTER 9

How Can I Train My Doberman Pinscher?

Brilliantly intelligent and eager to please, Doberman Pinschers are fast learners who welcome challenges. Bred to be working dogs, Dobermans are trainable and are happiest when they are kept busy. Their nimble minds are constantly working and looking for new learning opportunities. As soon as you bring your new little Doberman puppy home from the breeder, you should start his training and education. Being as strong and consistent trainer will show your Doberman, right from the very start, that you are the boss, not your dog.

Training your Doberman Pinscher can be divided into four different categories…obedience, correcting negative behavior, tricks, and working.

Obedience Training

There are some basic life skills that your Doberman needs to master as he becomes a member of your household. Fortunately, Dobermans are quick learners so if you start early and are consistent with your training, your little puppy should know how to properly behave in no time.

Your Doberman's first task will be housetraining. Until he is completely housebroken, you can put down puppy pads or spread around newspapers in hopes that he will do his business on these, rather than on your carpeting or furniture. Watch him closely and when you see him strike a pose, quickly move him to the newspaper or take him outside, all the while repeating the command you have chosen, such as "potty," "outside," or "poo-poo time." Soon your Doberman puppy will learn to connect the act of relieving himself with the command and the place. As he gets used to the puppy pads, transition him to go outside. Try to establish a consistent schedule for your Doberman puppy, so he is eating and going outside at predictable times. Despite all your efforts, your puppy will probably have occasional accidents in the house. As frustrating as this can be, refrain from punishing your pup. After all, he is still a baby, and he is trying to learn. Instead, offer praise and a treat if he successfully goes outside. Also, check to see if your behavior is the cause of his accidents…have you changed his schedule? Have you ignored his yapping at the door? Have you misinterpreted when he pawed at his newspaper? Did you fail to connect his pacing and anxiety to housetraining?

You will most likely want to crate train your Doberman Pinscher puppy, especially if you will be leaving him home alone while you are at work all day. Left to his own devices, your puppy may get into trouble. He may chew on your belongings and destroy household items. Crate training, like all types of training, needs to be consistently utilized to be the most effective. Many dog owners disapprove of crate training because they view it as a cruel cage, but most dogs quickly learned that their crate is their safe haven…the place where they can go to unwind and decompress. You should approach your dog's crate as his personal space, or bedroom. Fill it with soft, comfortable, washable bedding and a few doggie toys to make it a welcoming place. If you use a specific command, such as "crate," when you put your Doberman in his crate, he will quickly learn to go to his special place when asked. A word of caution about crate training…the crate should not be used as a doggie jail, a place to go as a form of punishment. You certainly don't want your Doberman to feel as though he is being punished every day when you crate him and leave for work.

Your Doberman will need to be on a leash when you have him out in public.

Leash training your Doberman should start as soon as he comes to live with you. Unless you have a fenced-in yard, most of the time that you have your Doberman outside, he will be on a leash, so he needs to learn how to behave properly on the leash. Eager

Doberman puppies will pull and strain against the leash. You should attach your Doberman's leash to a dog harness, rather than a collar, for the safety of your dog. Try clipping on the leash while you are at home and play with your Doberman puppy so that he starts to associate leash time with fun time. You can train your Doberman with a verbal command, such as "walk," "lead," or "leash," as you attach the leash so that he knows that leash time is coming.

Lastly, you need to train your Doberman Pinscher to come to you when you call his name, or issue a command, such as "here" or "come." This will prove invaluable if your puppy slips his leash while you are out for a walk and runs, excitedly, away from you. You should start this training as soon as possible. Get down on the floor with your puppy and call his name along with the "here" or "come" command. Take care to keep the tone of your voice happy, and upbeat…you don't want your puppy to associate his own name with being in trouble. If you need to get your distracted puppy's attention, clap your hands, then give your command. Reward him when he comes to you by giving him a belly rub, and ear scratch, or a small treat. Work on this lesson as often as necessary until you believe your Doberman puppy has it mastered. Then move the lesson to the outside or to an unfamiliar area and try it again. At first, he may be too distracted by the new surroundings to remember his training, but soon he will be back on track. In no time at all, you will be confident that your Doberman puppy will come to you when called.

Correcting Negative Behavior

Very quickly, your Doberman puppy may pick up some bad habits. Digging, begging, barking, chewing, jumping up on people, or showing aggression are all behaviors that can be corrected with strong and consistent training. The key is to establish yourself as the leader of the pack from day one. Dobermans are natural leaders, and they will try to assume the role of the boss if you let them. Once he learns his place, however, he will follow your commands. If your Doberman starts to demonstrate some negative behavior, you need to immediately nip it in the bud. The sooner he learns that his behavior is not to be tolerated, the sooner it can be corrected.

Dobermans are natural guard dogs, and they want to protect you and your family. Their bark can be scary and intimidating to people who are unfamiliar with the breed. You could try to reduce triggers that cause your dog to bark and increase the effect by rewarding your dog when he refrains from barking. Very quickly, your Doberman will figure out that when he barks, he gets ignored, but when he is silent, he is rewarded. Remember that Dobermans, like all dog breeds, respond best to positive reinforcement. You may be tempted to yell at your barking Doberman, or even threaten him, but doing so will not stop his negative habits. It will only make him afraid of you.

Chewing is a natural act for curious puppies. It is one way that they explore their world and eases the discomfort of teething. Teach your puppy a command, such as "stop" or "drop," if you catch him with your shoe, or TV remote, or headphones, so he learns that not everything within his reach is a chew toy. Providing him with an alternative to your shoes…plenty of doggie toys that he can chew on…will help relieve his chewing urges.

Today's Dobermans are less aggressive and generally calmer than Dobermans of several generations ago. They are no longer a fearsome aggressor. Your Doberman may react with a growl or a nip in situations where he feels threatened and is trying to protect you. If you have established yourself as the alpha in control, he will not feel as though the sole responsibility of protecting the family falls to him. If your dog does exhibit signs of aggression, use the commands he has learned to re-establish yourself as the leader and to calm him down. This will let him know that his aggressive behavior is not appropriate. As always, closely supervise your Doberman, and any dog, with children. Children may move quickly and act unexpectedly, which could trigger the Doberman's defensive nature.

Learning Tricks

Dobermans love to keep their minds active and challenged. They easily master basic dog tricks, such as "sit," "stay," and "shake," and are eager to learn more. Their intelligence, coupled with their athletic nature, make them perfect for agility and obedience training. Learning new tricks will help your Doberman Pinscher feel like he has a purpose in life, which will keep him happy and healthy.

Training for Work

Dobermans were bred to be working dogs, and they still retain that instinct. They have incredible endurance and athleticism, along with their superior intelligence. Dobermans make excellent police dogs, guard dogs, search and rescue dogs, leader dogs, and therapy dogs. Dobermans are employed at airports and military bases. Specific training for a particular job may require an expert dog trainer. Once a Doberman is well-trained in the basics… "sit," "stay," etc.… he can begin specialized training. Working Dobermans are an elite class of dogs. They are confident, hard-working, tenacious, and faithful.

CHAPTER 10

How Do I Keep My Doberman Pinscher Healthy?

When you bring a Doberman Pinscher into your life, you are making the commitment to take the best care of this dog. This means ensuring that he stays healthy and fit, so he can experience a high quality of life for years to come. The well-being and safety of your Doberman should be your main concern. In general, Dobermans are a healthy breed, but there are a few breed-specific health concerns you should be aware of. To stay on top of your Doberman's health, you should establish a rapport with your veterinarian, so the two of you can form a united team, devoted to your dog's medical care. Routine veterinarian check-ups are the first step.

Throughout this chapter, we will take a brief look at preventative medical care for your Doberman Pinscher, as well as common diseases and health problems to watch out for.

What Preventative Care and Vaccines Does My Doberman Pinscher Need?

Good preventative health care for your Doberman starts with vaccinations. This is for the protection of your dog and all the other dogs he may come into contact with. You should carefully and diligently follow the recommended vaccinations routine, as shown in the chart below. In addition to these required vaccinations that your dog must have, you should also check with your veterinarian. Some areas have additional vaccine requirements.

PUPPY AGE	RECOMMENDED VACCINES	OPTIONAL VACCINES
6-8 weeks	Distemper, measles, parainfluenza	Bordetella
10-12 weeks	DHPP (vaccines for distemper, adenovirus [hepatitis], parainfluenza, and parvovirus)	Coronavirus, Leptospirosis, Bordetella, Lyme disease
12-24 weeks	Rabies	None
14-16 weeks	DHPP	Coronavirus, Lyme disease, Leptospirosis
12-16 months	Rabies, DHPP	Coronavirus, Lyme disease, Leptospirosis
Every 1-2 years	DHPP	Coronavirus, Lyme disease, Leptospirosis
Every 1-3 years	Rabies (check local laws)	None

On the day that you pick up your Doberman puppy from the breeder, you will receive documentation about the vaccinations your puppy has been given. If the breeder doesn't offer this, ask. Then, take these documents to your veterinarian on your puppy's first visit, so that it can be put into his permanent healthcare record. Vaccines have been designed to control disease and work best when responsible pet owners stay current with the shots.

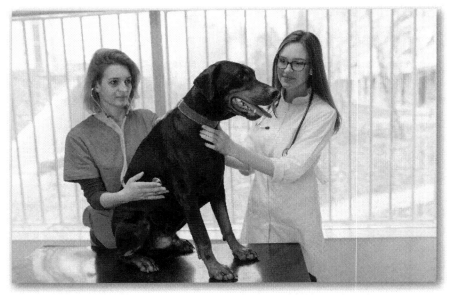

Routine veterinarian visits will help to keep your Doberman healthy and fit.

Doberman puppies inherit some antibodies from their mothers when they are born. These will protect them for the first eight weeks of their lives. After that, they need our help to keep them protected from common diseases. Vaccines are really just a suppressed or dead version of the disease that is injected into the dog. The disease is so weakened that it will not make the animal sick, but it will trigger an automatic response in the dog's immune system. Your Doberman will produce antibodies to fight off this specific disease. These antibodies lay in wait, prepared to engage in combat with the disease if it ever aggressively invades and attacks the body.

At the ages of seven weeks, ten weeks, thirteen weeks, and sixteen weeks, your Doberman puppy will need to have vaccinations for parvovirus, distemper, hepatitis, parainfluenza, and leptospirosis. These are typically combined into one injection, called a DHLP-P vaccination. In addition to the required vaccines, your puppy may need an inoculation for internasal bordetella, between the ages of eight and sixteen weeks if he was kept in a kennel with other dogs. The internasal bordetella vaccine protects the pup from a condition called kennel cough. If you plan to leave your Doberman at doggie daycare or an overnight kennel, you will be required to show proof of having the internasal bordetella vaccine. You will most likely need to repeat the internasal bordetella vaccine every six months if your puppy is in regular contact with other dogs…at doggie daycare, the dog park, or dog shows.

You will also need to get your Doberman puppy rabies vaccines, which are given between four and six months of age. After that initial injection, it will need a rabies shot on a yearly basis. Depending on where you live, you might also need to get a rabies booster shot for your pup, midway between the initial rabies injection and the second year one. Your veterinarian will be able to tell you if this booster is recommended for dogs living in your area.

You may also wish to vaccinate your Doberman puppy for some additional diseases, such as coronavirus and Lyme disease. Coronavirus is, itself, not serious or fatal to dogs, but it becomes dangerous if there are other conditions present, such as parvo.

Coronavirus leads to severe diarrhea in puppies, which, in turn, leads to dehydration. Lyme disease is associated with tick bites and can cause joint pain, stiffness, arthritis, and fatigue in dogs. It is dangerous, but typically not fatal to dogs. Lyme disease is treatable with a dose of antibiotics. One of the biggest issues with Lyme disease, however, is that it can flare back up periodically throughout the dog's life if the animal has not been vaccinated for it.

What Are Common Diseases Affecting Doberman Pinschers?

Wobbler's Syndrome

Wobbler's syndrome is the common name for a neurologic disease that afflicts the neck spine area, of large breed dogs. Other names for Wobbler's syndrome include cervical vertebral instability, cervical vertebral malformation, and cervical spondylopathy, among others.

Some of the symptoms of Wobbler's syndrome is a dog that walks with his head down...an indication the dog is in pain. You may also observe the dog having a wobbly gait and difficulty getting up after laying down. They may even appear to buckle over at the front knees.

Wobbler's syndrome most affects large breed dogs. In fact, roughly 96% of dogs diagnosed with the affliction are larger dogs. Dobermans, along with Great Danes, German Shepherds, Weimaraners, Mastiffs, and Bernese Mountain Dogs, are prone to the syndrome. The Veterinary Medical Databases indicate that the disease is present in 5.5% of Dobermans.

Dobermans diagnosed with Wobbler's disease are treated either with steroid or non-steroidal anti-inflammatory medications and limited activity. They can also be treated with surgery, depending on the severity of the symptoms. Because Wobbler's syndrome affects the neck area of the dog, Doberman owners should avoid using neck leashes and select chest harnesses instead.

Hip Dysplasia

Hip dysplasia is not uncommon in Doberman Pinschers. If your Doberman is slow to get up, reluctant to jump or refuses to climb stairs, it could be because he is experiencing pain in his hips due to hip dysplasia. Hip dysplasia is a malformation of the hip socket and is a genetic trait that is more prevalent in larger breed dogs. It is the number one cause of arthritis of the hips in dogs.

Hip dysplasia in Dobermans causes pain and stiffness and can greatly diminish your dog's everyday activities and overall quality of life. There are a few ways to treat hip dysplasia in Dobermans. Non-surgical treatment options involve anti-inflammatory and pain medications, limited exercise, and weight control. Adding a few extra pounds will just exasperate the pain and immobility. Additionally, it is important for the dog to stay active to keep his joints moving and to keep his weight down, but too much activity may cause him pain. Hip dysplasia can also be treated with surgery to repair or reshape the hip joint, allowing for a greater range of motion. Lastly, mesenchymal stem cell therapy has been used to treat the symptoms of hip dysplasia, particularly the osteoarthritis.

Von Willebrand's Disease

Von Willebrand's Disease is a blood disease that is caused by a deficiency of the von Willebrand Factor, an adhesive protein in the blood that is needed for platelet clotting, or coagulation. It is akin to hemophilia in humans and can cause excessive bleeding. Von Willebrand's disease is a genetic disorder that impacts certain dog breeds more than others. Unfortunately, Doberman Pinschers, as well as German Shepherds, Standard Poodles, Golden Retrievers, and Shetland Sheepdogs, are more apt to acquire von Willebrand's disease.

Symptoms of von Willebrand's disease include spontaneous nosebleeds, bloody urine or feces, bleeding from the gums, prolonged bleeding after an injury, and excessive bruising of the skin. Von Willebrand's disease is treated by blood transfusions as necessary and by taking preventative measures to lessen the chance of injury.

Gastric Torsion or Bloat

Gastric torsion, also known as bloat, is a very dangerous condition and can quickly escalate to a life-threatening situation in Dobermans. In fact, it is the second leading cause of death in dogs, second only to cancer. Bloat is caused by a build-up of gasses in the dog's stomach. The stomach can twist or rotate, which closes off the esophagus and intestines. The gas build-up has no way to escape. Immediate surgery is the only option at this point. If you suspect that your dog is experiencing gastric torsion, take him immediately to the veterinarian or emergency clinic. Time is of the essence.

Bloat is more common in dogs with deep chests, such as Dobermans, German Shepherds, and Great Danes. Symptoms of bloat include anxiety and nervousness, enlarged abdomen, and a hunched or arched posture. They may try to vomit, but nothing comes up or attempt to poop with no output.

Cardiomyopathy

Often called a silent killer, cardiomyopathy is a heart disease caused, in part, by abnormalities in the heart muscles. The condition causes the walls of the heart to become enlarged and weakened. Therefore, they cannot pump blood as effectively. Cardiomyopathy is a genetic disorder that affects some dog breeds more than others. The Doberman Pinscher, unfortunately, is one of those dog breeds, in which higher occurrences of cardiomyopathy are reported.

Symptoms of cardiomyopathy in Dobermans evolve as the disease progresses. In the beginning, your Doberman Pinscher may exhibit signs of weakness, fatigue, and lethargy. Later, he may cough and have shortness of breath as fluids back up into his lungs. He may then show signs of liver malfunction and abdominal distension.

There is no cure for cardiomyopathy in dogs, and for Dobermans, the long-term prognosis is not favorable. The goal of treatment is to keep the dog's heart functioning as normally as possible, for as long as possible. Your veterinarian can prescribe blood pressure medicine or other medications that can help normalize the dog's heartbeat and minimize fluid accumulation in the lungs.

Demodicosis

Better known as mange, demodicosis is an inflammatory skin disease caused by mites. Demodicosis can cause hair loss, lesions, self-biting, scaly skin, and immune system issues. Demodicosis can be widespread or localized and often inflicts the trunk and legs. In most milder cases of demodicosis, the conditions resolve themselves with time, but in more severe cases, long-term medication may be needed.

CHAPTER 11

What Do I Need to Know About Grooming My Doberman Pinscher?

D obermans require very little grooming to maintain their sleek and handsome coats. Their short fur is easy to keep clean and does not get dirty and smelly if they go a long time between baths. There are, however, a few routine tasks that will help to keep your Doberman looking his best.

Dobermans are low maintenance dogs but may need occasional baths.

79

Do Dobermans Need Frequent Brushing?

No. You can get away with brushing your Doberman as infrequently as once a week. His short, straight fur naturally repels dirt and doesn't knot up. Brushing will remove loose hair, so he doesn't shed on your carpet as much. Dobermans shed year-round. A good brushing will keep your Doberman's coat shiny and healthy.

The close-cropped coat of the Doberman doesn't require thick dog brushes that other breeds may need. In fact, Doberman grooming tools can be kept to a minimum. You can use a soft finishing brush on your Doberman, or even a rubber curry brush. Some Doberman owners swear by pumice stones, typically used to brush horses, as an effective tool for removing excess hair.

Do Dobermans Require Frequent Bathing?

Again, no. Dobermans are clean animals, and their short fur does not hold dirt and odors. Many Doberman owners claim they only bathe their dogs a few times per year. Instead of a typical bath, you can wipe down your Doberman Pinscher with a damp towel to remove surface dirt or loose hairs. Occasionally, a bath is necessary. Your Doberman may decide to play in the mud, or roll in a foul-smelling substance, making a good bath a necessity. You can wash his fur using a gentle dog shampoo that you thoroughly rinse out. Afterward, you simply need to towel dry his coat, and he will be good as new.

What Do I Need to Know About Doberman Nail Care?

Like most dog breeds, Doberman Pinscher nail care includes monthly nail clipping. If your Doberman spends plenty of time outside and can run on rough surfaces, his nails make stay short, but if your dog cannot keep his nails trimmed naturally, you will need to clip them every three or four weeks. Nails that become too long can cause pain when your dog steps, therefore you should inspect his nails on a regular basis and clip them as needed.

Doberman nail clippers should be strong, durable, and sharp enough, to quickly and easily cut his tough and thick nails. As an alternative, you can use a Dremel tool (small electric rotating grinder) to smoothly trim your dog's nails. If the dog's nails have gotten too long, clipping them may be difficult (for you and the dog!), and can result in the nail splitting. Grinding them down with a Dremel dog trimming tool may be more effective.

What Should I Know About Doberman Ear Care?

When you brush your Doberman, take a moment to inspect his ears. If you see any signs of infection or irritation, or if there is an excess of waxy build-up or a strange odor, schedule a veterinarian appointment for your Doberman Pinscher. Do not attempt to clean out his ears yourself with a cotton swab or any other device. You can easily damage your dog's sensitive ears. Leave the internal ear care to the experts. You can, however, clean the external ear flap yourself, as needed, using a dampened cotton ball or a soft washcloth.

What Should I Know About Doberman Eye Care?

Dobermans are prone to producing secretions from their eyes, which dry into a crust. Some dogs produce more than others. Most of the time, the Doberman Pinscher will rub the crust away himself...probably, onto your carpet or couch! If not, you may have to help him out. It is an easy task. Simply take a tissue and wipe the dog's eyelids in an outward direction. Do not touch the animal's eyeball as you may scratch it or cause irritation.

What Should I Know About Doberman Dental Care?

From an early age, you should get into the habit of looking into your Doberman's mouth to check his teeth. If you start when he is a puppy, he will get accustomed to this and will be cooperative and docile. You should ensure that your Doberman Pinscher's teeth remain strong and healthy throughout his life because dental diseases can spread to the dog's internal organs and cause damage. For this reason, many veterinarians recommend that you brush your dog's teeth on a daily basis. To do this, use a dog toothbrush and dog toothpaste that is specifically made for larger breed dogs. Never use human toothpaste, as this can be toxic to dogs. When you brush your Doberman's teeth, just brush the outside of the teeth in a back and forth motion. Don't try to brush the inside of the dog's teeth…you may hurt the animal's gums or mouth. He will keep the inside of his teeth clean using his tongue.

CHAPTER 12

What Do I Need to Know About Ear Cropping and Tail Docking in Dobermans?

C ertain purebred dogs, including the Doberman Pinscher, are commonly subjected to not one, but two, elective surgical procedures while still in the puppy stage. These surgeries – tail docking and ear cropping – are nearly as old as the dog breed itself and, although a widespread practice, has become rather controversial.

Why are Dobermans' Ears Cropped?

Cropping the ears of the Doberman Pinscher was originally done give the animal an imposing and sleek appearance, protect the dog's ears when the animal was hunting, to improve hearing, and for health reasons. Dobermans were bred for protection, so their ears were cropped so that they wouldn't become a target for attacking animals that can easily bite and rip them. Dobermans are also active, athletic dogs; therefore, it was believed that the Doberman's natural ears would snag on branches and brush, and cause injuries to the dog.

Early breeders of the Doberman Pinscher were also under the assumption that erect ears meant an increase in hearing. For guard dogs such as Doberman Pinschers, the ability to detect threatening sounds was vitally important.

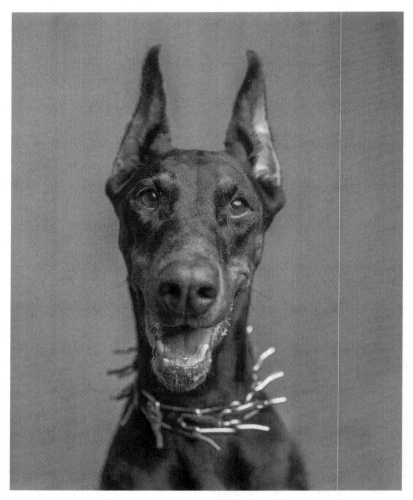

Cropped ears stand erect on a Doberman.

Another reason for cropping Dobermans ears was to keep them free of infection. It was believed that the heavy, drooping dog ears would trap moisture and cause infections. Dobermans ears, however, are not as heavy and thick as other dog breeds, so they tend to stay cleaner and freer of infection than other breeds. In general, though, dogs with cropped ears have fewer infections and ear problems, then uncropped dogs.

When and How are Dobermans Ears Cropped?

Most veterinarians recommend that the Doberman be between the ages of 7 and 9 weeks when they have the ear cropping procedure done. The surgery should only be done by a veterinarian who is experienced in the process. The dog is sedated and put under using anesthesia. The ears are trimmed and taped to stand erect. The entire procedure takes about thirty minutes.

After-surgery care involves keeping the ears taped for 5 or 6 months until the ears stand upright on their own. Dog owners need to be diligent about keeping the ears clean and dry, to prevent infections and injury. A roughhousing puppy may damage his healing ears.

Is Doberman Ear Cropping Legal?

Ear cropping is not legal in all countries, in part because many people view the practice as cruel and unnecessary. Animal rights groups have lobbied for laws to be passed in several countries, in regard to ear cropping in dogs. In England, it is illegal to crop the ears of all dogs, and dogs with cropped ears are banned from competing in British Kennel Club sanctioned dog shows and agility events. In Germany, where the Doberman breed originated, ear cropping is strictly banned, as it is in Australia, New Zealand, Sweden, and Norway. Several Canadian provinces have prohibited ear cropping, either through provincial law or through regulatory bylaws. In the United States, however, there is not a nationwide ban on the practice of ear cropping. In fact, the American Kennel Club encourages the continuation of the practice.

Why are Dobermans' Tails Docked?

The traditional school of thought advocates for tail docking in Doberman Pinschers, primarily because records show that Louis Doberman wanted that streamlined appearance to the dog he developed. Additionally, tail docking was a common practice for working dogs, the class of dog to which the Doberman belongs. When working-class dogs are working, the tail can be a hindrance. For a guard dog like the Doberman, the tail could be bitten or pulled by an attacker. Doberman tails, when they are undocked and fully grown, can be somewhat fragile and prone to injuries and breaks. For these reasons, proponents of tail docking in Doberman Pinschers claim the practice is done for the safety and benefit of the dog. People against the practice of docking, however, view it as an unneeded and harmful procedure that is cruel to the animal.

When and How are Dobermans' Tails Docked?

Tails are docked in Dobermans when they are still very young puppies, typically between 3 and 5 days old. Most often, the tail docking is done by the breeder who clamps a band around the puppy's tail. The band cuts off the flow of blood to the tail, and the appendage dies and falls off on its own several days later.

The current push is for the procedure to be done by a licensed veterinarian in a clean and sterile setting, rather than in a breeder's backyard or kennel. Either way, aftercare is important to ensure that the site stays clean and infection-free.

Is Doberman Tail Docking Legal?

Like ear cropping, tail docking in the United States is common practice with almost no restrictions. Instead, the American Kennel Club's breed standards for the Doberman Pinscher require docked tails. Conversely, tail docking is absolutely prohibited in England, Wales, Australia, Greece, Switzerland, Norway, and Ireland. Only working-class dogs are exempt from tail docking bans in England, Wales, Germany, and Denmark. The legality of tail docking varies from province to province in Canada, with no national law addressing the practice.

CHAPTER 13

Should I Show My Doberman Pinscher?

One way to connect with other Doberman Pinscher owners in your area and to compare your Doberman with the breed standards for the dog is to participate in dog shows. Dog shows exist as a way for fanciers to judge the breeding stock of a specific breed of dog. Therefore the dogs that are shown in dog shows cannot have been spayed or neutered. The animal is rated on its ability to produce a top-quality litter of puppies. The dogs are not judged against each other, but rather against the breed standards for the animal. Learning a bit more about dog shows will help you decide if you and your dog should participate in dog shows.

Dog shows are organized and hosted by local, regional, and national dog breed clubs. Breed clubs maintain the breed standards for each dog breed in its club. Your first step in participating in the dog show experience is to connect with a breed club. The breeder who sold you your Doberman Pinscher may be able to put you in touch with a local or regional breed club. The club will be able to provide you with resources to help you raise a healthy, happy dog, but also give you information about breed standards and upcoming dog shows.

Dog shows are a wonderful way to meet more Doberman fans.

If your goal is to enter your Doberman in dog shows, you need to be sure you select a superior puppy when you are puppy shopping. You will need a purebred dog that is registered with the national kennel club of your country. Your dog will need to remain unaltered – not neutered or spayed—and stay current on vaccines. If you live in the United States, you will be required to have your Doberman's ears cropped, and tail docked, in order to comply with the American Kennel Club standards. Dobermans with natural ears and tails can, however, participate in dog shows in nearly every other country because ear cropping and tail docking procedure have been phased out as a common practice. Most kennel clubs recognize four acceptable coat colors for the

Doberman Pinscher – black and rust, blue and rust, fawn and rust, and red and rust.

When entering a dog show, you should know what class the Doberman Pinscher belongs to. The Kennel Club UK divides dog breeds into seven groups – the terrier group, the hound group, the working group, the pastoral group, the utility group, the gundog group, and the toy group. The Canadian Kennel Club also has seven classifications – the sporting group, the non-sporting group, the working group, the toy group, the herding group, hounds, and terriers. There are, however, eight classifications within the American Kennel Club -- the hound group, the terrier group, the toy group, the sporting group, the non-sporting group, the working group, the herding group, and the miscellaneous group. The national kennel clubs of both Australia and New Zealand recognize seven groups – toys, terriers, hounds, gundogs, working dogs, utility dogs, and non-sporting dogs. In the American Kennel Club, Canadian Kennel Club, and the Kennel Club UK, the Doberman Pinscher is a member of the working class. But Dobermans belong to the utility class in the Australian Kennel Club and the New Zealand Kennel Club.

If you decide you want to show your Doberman Pinscher, you should train your dog from an early age and work with him to prepare him for the show ring. You must also make the commitment to keeping him fit and active, as well as feeding him high-quality food for optimal health and body stature. If you want your dog to be competitive in dog shows, you will need to invest the time, energy, and money to make it a success. Participating in showing your dog can be a pleasurable hobby for you and your dog, and help you meet other Doberman lovers.

CHAPTER 14

What Do I Need to Know About Doberman Pinscher Breeding, Pregnancy, and Birth?

I f you have fallen in love with the Doberman Pinscher breed and you are smitten with your own Doberman dog, you may decide to breed your dog. If you do, there is much to learn. First and foremost, you want to breed your Doberman in a responsible way. You owe it to the Dobermans to practice safe breeding while keeping the integrity of the breed intact. Additionally, you will need to know about finding a mate, the Doberman Pinscher heat cycle, how to care for a pregnant Doberman, how to prepare for the birth of the puppies, and how to care for the newborn puppies.

How Do I Find a Mate for My Doberman Pinscher?

Obviously, before you can breed your Doberman, you need to find a mate. If you own two Dobermans with different parentage, you can breed them together, but most of the time, a Doberman owner needs to find a suitable mate. It can be challenging to find a mate that meets your criteria, and you should be sure to take your time and be sure that you are picking a mate with desirable traits. The bitch, or female Doberman, or sire, or male Doberman, that you select should be in good health and be registered with your country's kennel club. You can talk to your veterinarian about your search for a suitable mate or check with a local or regional Doberman breed club. Either source may be able to put you in touch with a Doberman owner who might be able to help you.

What is the Doberman Pinscher Heat Cycle?

After you have made your decision about a suitable mate, you need to ensure that the female Doberman is fertile. Observe her so you can follow her heat cycle. Intact female Dobermans can experience their first heat between the age of 5 to 14 months, and after that, will come into season, or heat, every 6 months on average. Each heat cycle lasts between 12 and 21 days. About 10 to 14 days into her cycle, after her discharge becomes clear, the female enters her fertile period.

A female dog in heat gives off a scent that attracts male dogs of any breed. Take care to keep you female Doberman in a secure place during her heat cycle so that she is not impregnated by neighborhood dogs. Puppies in the same litter can have different fathers if the mother has mated with several different dogs, but the integrity of the entire litter is compromised. None of the puppies can be considered purebred. For this reason, you need to safeguard your female Doberman when she is in heat. Male dogs who catch her scent will aggressively try to reach her and mate with her.

What Should I Know About Doberman Pinschers Mating?

Wait to put the male and female Dobermans together until you believe the female is in her fertility stage. You can either ask your veterinarian to check her hormone levels, or you can do the less-reliable 'flags" test. Simply scratch the female's fur at the base of her tail. If she is fertile and ready to mate, she will lift her tail involuntarily and twitch it from side to side, like she is waving a flag to alert potential mates. If you put the male and female Dobermans together before the female is ready to mate, the two may fight. The hormone scents given off by the female will excite and agitate the male, causing even the most docile Dobermans to react aggressively.

When it is mating time, there is very little you have to do. The dogs can handle things without human interference. All you need to do is bring the male Doberman to the female's kennel and watch for mating to occur. While it is possible for the female Doberman to get pregnant after just one mating, you should allow them to mate several times, just to be sure. You can put the dogs together every other day throughout the female's fertility cycle. You will know when she is no longer fertile when she refuses to mate anymore. Watch her closely for clues. When she says "no," it is time to put a halt to the mating arrangements.

What Do I Need to Know About Doberman Pinscher Pregnancy?

You will know for sure if your Doberman Pinscher is pregnant about a month after mating has occurred. She will gain weight and have protruding nipples and may want to eat more. If you

93

are still unsure if your Doberman female is pregnant, or you want to rule out a false pregnancy, you could ask your veterinarian to perform a doggie ultrasound. This will give you a glimpse inside her uterus and may even let you know how many puppies to expect.

The gestational period for Doberman Pinschers is about 65 days. During her pregnancy, it is your task to make the female comfortable and well-fed. You should discuss her changing nutritional requirements with your veterinarian, who may recommend increasing her calorie intake, as well as her protein and fat intake. To stay fit, you want your Doberman to mother-to-be to remain active, but you should take care that she doesn't overdo it.

How Do I Prepare for My Doberman Pinscher to Give Birth?

You have most likely done your math and have a date circled on the calendar. Of course, puppies come when they want to come, regardless of what the calendar says, so you should be sure to plan for labor and delivery, well in advance.

You can prepare a birthing area for her, by making a large box or crate lined with newspaper and topped with soft, washable blankets available. The birthing box should be situated in a quiet part of the house, away from the hustle and bustle of everyday activities. Introduce your Doberman to her birthing area well in advance of her due date, so she has time to become familiar with it. She needs to feel that it is a safe and secure place for her puppies, or she won't use it. Instead, she may choose to have her babies in a closet, or on a pile of laundry, or on your bed. Do what you can to acclimate her to the birthing box, so you don't find a litter of puppies in a strange place in your home.

Doberman puppies start little but grow fast.

If you suspect that your female Doberman is starting labor, you can gently encourage her to go to her birthing box. She may, however, become agitated and want to move to a different spot. This is a sign that she doesn't feel entirely comfortable in the location you have chosen. Don't force her to stay. This will only create undue stress during the birth process.

What Do I Need to Know About Doberman Pinscher Labor and Delivery?

As your Doberman mother-to-be's due date nears, watch for physical signs that labor is beginning. She may become restless or anxious or start pacing and panting. She may lick herself or start nesting…rearranging her bedding material. She will probably want to be left alone. This may be hard for you and your family because you don't want to miss the big event but try to give her privacy. If you have been taking your Doberman's temperature throughout her pregnancy, you will notice that her normal body temperature is 105.5 degrees Fahrenheit. As labor starts, however, your Doberman's body temperature will go down to 101 or 100 degrees.

Your Doberman really doesn't need any help during labor and delivery. After all, it is a natural process. Dogs have been having puppies for a long, long time without any interference from humans. If your dog appears to shiver during labor, don't be concerned. She is not too cold; it is just her body's way of regulating her body during contractions. If you watch her flanks, you may see her uterus contracting. You will also, most likely, notice a discharge from her genital area.

If you stay with your Doberman to watch the miracle of birth, you should try to be as unobtrusive as possible. It is exciting, but try to control yourself, so you do not exclaim loudly when a puppy appears. Rather, speak calmly and low to your Doberman, offering praise and encouragement.

The average Doberman Pinscher litter size is about 6 puppies. Typically, they are born about twenty minutes apart. Don't be surprised, however, if she takes a break for an hour or two, midway through the process. It is called "labor" because it is hard work. In all, it could take between 3 and 12 hours to birth all the puppies.

As each puppy makes his grand arrival into the world, the mother Doberman will gnaw through the umbilical cord and the sac, then lick the puppy clean. If she isn't finished with one puppy when another one arrives, don't worry, or jump in to help. The mother will return to the task at hand, as soon as she can. You may see some puppies appear tail first. That is not uncommon, and no cause for alarm.

How Do I Care for Newborn Doberman Pinscher Puppies?

When you are sure that all the Doberman pups have been delivered, offer the new mama some food and water and the opportunity to go outside to relieve her bladder. If she refuses to go, it could be that she feels as though her puppies are not safe alone. You and the rest of the family should leave the room. This will give the mother some alone time with her babies and a chance to see that it is safe for her to leave them for a few moments. Don't rush it, but as soon as you can, you should remove the soiled bedding and replace it with clean, dry bedding.

The Doberman puppies will be small and helpless for the first few weeks. Most of their time will be spent nursing, sleeping, and bonding with their mother and litter mates. In no time at all, the pups will be big enough for playing and running about. All Doberman puppies are adorable, but young puppies just learning to walk and run, will definitely melt your heart.

As much as you may want to, you cannot keep all of the puppies. Ideally, you would have started looking for good homes for most of them before they were even born, but if not, you need to work on securing them new owners by the time they are 8 weeks old. You can ask at your veterinarian's office or your local Doberman Pinscher club to see if you can get the word out about your puppies. Before you send them off into the world, your Doberman pups will need their first veterinarian visit and the first round of vaccines.

CHAPTER 15

Are Miniature Pinschers a Smaller Version of Doberman Pinschers?

The Miniature Pinscher looks a lot like the Doberman Pinscher. They both have muscular, compact bodies with short, smooth coats. Both are most commonly found with black fur trimmed in rust or brown. Both are active and intelligent dogs with a playful, curious personality. There is one marked difference, though. The Miniature Pinscher, also known as the Min Pin, is less than half the size of a Doberman, standing only about 10 inches tall (25.4 centimeters). Since the two dog breeds look so much alike, it is easy to see why many people assume the Min Pin is a miniature version of the Doberman Pinscher. In this chapter, we will take a brief look at the Miniature Pinscher and explore the relationship between this dog and the Doberman.

What is the History of Mini Pinschers?

Like all dog breeds, the Miniature Pinscher and the Doberman Pinscher are related. But are Min Pins a diminutive, or toy form of the standard Doberman Pinscher? The answer to this question is no. Although the precise origins of both breeds of dog are unclear, we do know that the Doberman and the Min Pin have different histories. Most dog breed experts agree that the Doberman Pinscher was not bred down to create the Miniature Pinscher, yet a few theorize that the opposite may have occurred. The Min Pin may have been bred up, to develop the Doberman. The Miniature Pinscher is an older breed than the Doberman, so this theory may hold water.

The word "Pinscher" means "terrier" in German. Therefore it is often assumed that both the Doberman Pinscher and the Miniature Pinscher originated in Germany. There is evidence, however, that the Min Pin was developed in Italy, or possibly in a Scandinavian country, at least one hundred years before the Doberman was developed. Some claim the Min Pin was the result of breeding an Italian Greyhound, a Dachshund, and some type of small, smooth-coated terrier, perhaps a German Pinscher or a Scandinavian Klein Pinscher.

Although we know that the Doberman was developed in Germany by Louis Doberman, we are unclear of the mix of dogs that make up the Doberman. A busy tax collector and kennel-owner, as we learned earlier, Herr Doberman did not keep good records of his breeding efforts while developing his namesake dog breed. Most experts believe that Herr Doberman crossed Great Danes, German Pinschers, and Rottweilers, but it is entirely possible that he added the Miniature Pinscher to the mix.

What are the Similarities Between the Doberman Pinscher and the Miniature Pinscher?

Clearly, both breeds of dog look alike. They have similar markings in the same coat color combinations: black and rust, black and tan, chocolate and tan, and rust. Their fur is short, straight, and glossy and they require very little maintenance and grooming to keep them looking sharp. Both the Doberman and the Min Pin have alert, erect ears, and well-sculpted, muscular bodies.

The Min Pin and the Doberman are also similar in temperament. Both breeds are highly active and athletic, requiring lots of exercise on a daily basis. They have higher than average energy levels and are happiest when they are kept busy. Neither breed of dog is designed to be a lap dog. Confident and loyal, both the Miniature Pinscher and the Doberman are protective watchdogs, although the Min Pin may not be as intimidating as the Doberman. The Min Pin, however, doesn't realize he is small. He is just as feisty as a much bigger dog, and you won't see a Miniature Pinscher backing down from a fight. Both breeds are noted for their high intelligence. You will continually be amazed at how smart these dogs are and the things they learn on their own.

What are the Differences between the Miniature Pinscher and the Doberman Pinscher?

Size is the biggest difference between the Miniature Pinscher and the Doberman Pinscher. The Min Pin weighs, on average, 7 to 11 pounds (3.175 to 4.989 kilograms) ...considerably less than the 60 to 90 pounds (27.215 to 40.823 kilograms) that the

Doberman weighs. Dobermans can stand 24 to 28 inches tall (61 to 72 centimeters), as compared to the 10 inches (25 centimeters) of the Min Pin.

Although both breeds of dogs are active, the smaller stature of the Miniature Pinscher makes it better suited for apartment living than the large and imposing Doberman.

The lifespan of a Miniature Pinscher is, on average, a bit longer than that of a Doberman. The difference can be attributed to the size discrepancies. Larger dog breeds tend to have a slightly shorter lifespan. You can expect a Min Pin to live to between 12 and 14 years of age, while a Doberman may only enjoy 10 to 12 years. Some of the health issues that Doberman may experience, as related to their size, such as hip dysplasia, is not as common in the smaller Min Pin. Likewise, the Min Pin breed may see an increased occurrence in other health issues, more prevalent in smaller dog breeds.

Should I Get a Doberman Pinscher or a Miniature Pinscher?

Selecting which breed is best for you is a matter of personal preference. You need to take into consideration your lifestyle, your family, your living arrangements, and then factor in how much time, money, and energy you must devote to your dog. You need to be committed to the animal and provide strong, consistent leadership, to whichever dog breed you choose.

CHAPTER 16

What Are Common Doberman Pinscher Mixes?

A Doberman Pinscher is definitely dramatic in appearance but is a big sweetheart. Their size and disposition make them popular for mixed breeding. Mixed breed dogs, under the name of designer dogs, are enjoying a rise in popularity in the last few years. Designer dogs are a controlled form of mix breeding by reputable breeders, who are breeding for specific qualities and physical features. The difference between commonly mixed dogs, or mutts, and designer dogs is that the breeders breed for consistent qualities. Therefore the majority of those mixes are similar in personality and physical characteristics. Doberman Pinscher mixes make terrific companion and family dogs, as well as working dogs. In this chapter, we take a brief look at some of the common Doberman mixes – with their catchy blended names – and the benefits of these designer mixed breeds.

Rotterman

Rottermans are crosses between Dobermans and Rottweilers. They are big, powerful dogs that need an owner who is a strong person who can keep the Rotterman in place. Rottermans get their protective nature from the Doberman parent. They can be counted on to watch over their families. They are also affectionate, despite their imposing appearance, and intelligent dogs that are easily trained. In fact, they make great working dogs and excel in search and rescue.

Doberdane

A newcomer to the designer dog roster, the Doberdane takes the best qualities of the Doberman Pinscher and combines them with the Great Dane to create a truly magnificent dog. These are powerful giants that need an experienced owner with strong and consistent training strategies. Therefore they are not recommended for first-time dog owners. But once you get past their formidable appearance, you will find the Doberdane is a wonderfully smart, agile, active, loving and loyal dog, that makes a great companion dog or therapy dog.

Beagleman

Sometimes called a Dobeagle, the Beagleman is a mix between a Doberman Pinscher and a Beagle. The Beagleman is typically smaller than your average Doberman, but is alert and protective, just like the Doberman. The Beagleman is a very active dog who need a lot of attention and exercise, yet their smaller stature means they can adapt to apartment living. They tend to be vocal dogs and will alert the family to any perceived threat by barking. Although Beagleman love to play with the family, they also make good tracking dogs.

Dobie

Calm, relaxed, friendly, and loving – that describes the Dobie, a cross between a Doberman Pinscher and a Collie. Unlike its Doberman parent, the Dobie is not a highly active dog. Rather than running around, it prefers to lie at your feet and soak up all your attention. In fact, they sometimes have a jealousy problem. Generally speaking, the Dobie looks like a medium sized Doberman but is not as well-defined and muscular. The face more closely resembles the collie, and the ears looked like uncropped Doberman ears. Dobies are not as vocal as other Doberman mixes, preferring to howl, rather than bark.

Doberhound

The best of the Doberman and the best of the Greyhound combine to create the Doberhound, a fairly new designer mixed breed dog that was created strictly to be a companion animal. Doberhounds are high energy dogs, after all, they were bred by crossing the Greyhound, a racing dog build for speed, with a Doberman Pinscher, an athletic dog built for protection. Doberhounds thrive as a member of an active family with plenty of room to run and play. Friendly and gentle giants, the Doberhounds generally get along well with children and other pets.

Doodleman

Doodleman, or Doodleman Pinschers, are created by breeding Doberman Pinschers with Standard Poodles. What is produced is a puppy with adorable, thick, curly fur in nearly any color.

They require more grooming and maintenance then purebred Dobermans. Averaging about 75 pounds (34.01 kilograms), the Doodleman can be stubborn but can be trained with firm, yet consistent training techniques and positive reinforcement. Doodleman dogs need space to run and explore but will love to include their human family in their play.

Doberman Shepherd

Doberman Pinschers are intimidating guard dogs, just like the German Shepherd, so it makes sense to cross the two dog breeds together to produce a Doberman Shepherd, a large and imposing hybrid. Doberman Shepherds need significant exercise on a daily basis…simply letting them roam the backyard, is not enough. So much power and stored energy needs to be made available, keep the Doberman Shepherd fit and in tip-top shape. This can be a big time commitment on the part of the dog's owner. Also, Doberman Shepherds are extremely smart, yet stubborn. They need an experienced owner who can demonstrate that he is the boss, not the dog.

CHAPTER 17

How Do I Care for My Aging Doberman Pinscher?

Doberman Pinschers, along with several other larger breed dogs, have a shorter lifespan than smaller dogs. The average life expectancy of a Doberman Pinscher is between 10 and 13 years. That means they begin to enter their golden years around 7 years of age. Your Doberman will experience changes in his body, mind, and personality as the aging process progresses. By understating these changes and knowing what warning signs to look for, you can be ready to help keep your Doberman healthy, active, and happy through his senior years. This chapter explains several of these changes – changes to his eating habits, joint stiffness, vision problems, and memory loss – that your Doberman Pinscher may encounter as he adds more birthdays.

How Will My Doberman's Diet and Nutritional Needs Change as He Ages?

The aging process tends to slow down even active dogs like the Doberman Pinscher. Less physical exercise means your dog may put on a few extra pounds. If this is the case, you will need to adjust his diet. Instead of feeding him less of his adult dog food, consult with your veterinarian or pet nutritionist about switching him to a senior formula dog food, that is specially designed for older dogs. Typically, senior formula dog foods have fewer calories, and the nutrients have been tweaked to accommodate the senior dog's needs. Staying fit and shedding that extra weight is an important step in keeping your older Doberman active and healthy. Studies have shown that overweight dogs age faster than trim and fit dogs, so staying in shape may help lengthen his life expectancy.

Older dogs may also run the risk of losing too much weight as they age. Your older Doberman may lose interest in his food or have difficulty chewing because of dental or digestive problems. Again, you should discuss these changes with your trusted veterinarian. Perhaps he or she will suggest switching your Doberman to a diet of wet or canned dog food, which is easier to eat for some older dogs.

How Will My Doberman's Water Needs and Kidney Functions Change as He Ages?

Your aging Doberman Pinscher may start drinking more water than normal as he gets older. A decrease in kidney function or the onset of conditions such as diabetes may cause an increase in thirst. Of course, as your Doberman drinks more water, he will urinate more. Your normally well-trained dog may start to have accidents in the house. Incontinence is more prevalent in female Dobermans that have been spayed because bladder function is linked to a decrease in estrogen production. Your female Doberman may also have little leaks when she sleeps or gets excited. Again, this is due to the loss of muscle tone in the bladder as a result of declining estrogen. Male Dobermans may also experience occasional bladder leaks.

As annoying and frustrating as this may be, keep in mind that it is not your Doberman's fault. He or she simply lacks the bladder control they had in their youth. Your Doberman is not mad at you, or trying to be naughty, or trying to send you a message. She should not be punished for something she cannot control. Instead, take her outside more often or place puppy pads on the floor. Bladder control issues could also be a sign of illness. Therefore you should schedule a check-up with your veterinarian to discuss your Doberman's incontinence problem, and rule out any underlying medical conditions.

Will My Doberman Experience Joint Pain and Stiffness as He Ages?

All dogs, including Doberman Pinschers, may experience joint pain and stiffness as a natural side effect of the aging process. Even we humans experience it! Your Doberman, once a fine athlete, may be slower to get up in the morning and appear stiff after a long nap. He may not have a spring in his step and may be reluctant to jump up into the car or climb stairs. If you believe your Doberman is in pain or discomfort from joint pain or stiffness, you should plan a visit to your veterinarian to discuss the situation. Your veterinarian can determine if the discomfort is caused by arthritis, hip dysplasia, or another cause, and prescribe appropriate medication to help alleviate his pain and inflammation.

Dobermans are accustomed to working hard, and your Doberman dog will carry that mindset into his golden years. He may act like he wants to join you on a long run or strenuous activity…and he may act just fine while he's doing it. But he may not know his new limitations and could easily overdo it. You may notice that it takes him longer to recover from a lot of activity. He may move slower the next day. You shouldn't stop all physical activity with your aging Doberman, but you should cut down gradually over time. Maybe the run or walk could be a bit shorter, or you could stop throwing the ball or Frisbee as many times. If you observe labored breathing, a change in your Doberman's gait, or other signs of fatigue or discomfort, give your dog a break or stop the activity.

Often, medium and larger breed dogs feel joint pain in their hips and hind legs first. You may notice that your Doberman is a bit unsteady when he gets up from a sitting position. If he has been allowed to get on the furniture, he may now seem reluctant to jump up on the couch or bed. You may need to give him a boost to help him get into his favorite spots without injuring himself. You could also consider buying a doggie ramp, sold at most pet stores, so your senior dog can climb up and down safely and with little pain.

How Will My Senior Doberman's Personality and Disposition Change?

As your Doberman Pinscher gets older, you may notice personality changes. Your Doberman may be irritable and cranky, and he may not be as patient and tolerant, as he normally was before. Changes in personality and temperament are a normal part of the aging process. Because you may not know how your Doberman will react to unfamiliar situations, such as encounters with strangers, other dogs, and small children, you need to watch your dog closely. Also, take necessary precautions to reduce triggers and stress to keep your Doberman from becoming snappish as he ages.

Will My Doberman Experience Vision and Hearing Problems?

Vision and hearing may decline as your Doberman ages. In fact, some elderly Dobermans can become totally blind or deaf. If you believe your Doberman is experiencing a decline in hearing or vision, you should discuss your concerns with your veterinarian. He or she will be able to rule out a more serious condition and give you treatment options. Depending on the underlying cause of the vision or hearing loss, there may be treatment options or, at the very least, ways to slow the progression. It is possible, though, for a blind or deaf dog to lead a normal, happy life. It will mean, however, that you will need to take care to reduce the chances for him to get hurt. Keep him on a leash when you are outside or at the dog park, and watch him closely. He may become startled by the unfamiliar, and lash out aggressively. Verbally warn him when a person or another dog approaches, so your Doberman doesn't perceive them as a threat. If your dog's hearing is declining, remember that he may not hear your commands, or hear you calling his name. At home, keep his surroundings as unchanged as possible. Rearranging the furniture will lead to confusion…and your Doberman bumping into the furniture.

Will My Doberman Experience Memory Loss and Confusion?

Memory loss is a sad but common part of the aging process. You may notice that your Doberman Pinscher is ignoring your commands. It is likely because he doesn't remember what the command means, not that he is being defiant. Don't punish him for his forgetfulness…he is not being bad or stubborn. He just finds it challenging to remember things he was taught a long time ago. Instead of expecting him to be able to recall his whole bag of tricks, stick to a few simple commands. Rewards him with generous amounts of attention and a treat if he does the trick, but he also deserves some love and cuddles if he gets it wrong. After all, he still wants to please you and be your loyal companion, even if he gets confused sometimes.

During his senior years, your Doberman Pinscher may need a bit more attention, a bit more veterinarian visits, and a bit more patience. If you got your Doberman as a young puppy, remember that you have been his lifelong companion. You owe it to him to reward his loyalty and faithfulness by making his golden years as happy and comfortable as you can.

CHAPTER 18

Conclusion

Strong, athletic, and intelligent, the Doberman Pinscher may have once had a reputation as an aggressive dog, but that stereotype is fading. Today, dog lovers realize that underneath his impressive and imposing exterior, the Doberman is a loyal, loving, playful companion that makes a wonderful addition to your family. The Doberman is an elite athlete and must be properly fed and exercised in order for him to stay at the top of his game. This muscle-bound jock is also exceptionally intelligent. He wants to be challenged physically and mentally.

Fit, trim, and commanding, your Doberman will get a lot of attention when you take him for walks or to the dog park. Although you want him to run and play, he will do so while keeping a sharp eye and ear alert for potential threats. He is, after all, a consummate guard dog and protector. His breed is used to being the top dog, so your Doberman will need a strong, consistent owner who can firmly lead the Doberman to know who is in charge. Once he figures out his place in your pack, he is happy to listen to the leader and follow instructions.

Regal and majestic, the Doberman is certainly a unique dog.

Dobermans, for the most part, enjoy few health issues. You can reduce the chances of your Doberman having serious medical problems by, first, purchasing your animal from a responsible breeder who has taken steps to make sure your dog has the best start in life. Second, you need to stay on top of your dog's preventative care by scheduling regular veterinarian visits and check-ups, heading the advice of your veterinarian or pet nutritionist, and staying current with all recommended vaccinations. The proper quantity and quality of dog food are also important for maintaining the health of your Doberman Pinscher.

Dobermans are working dogs. Bred to be protective watchdogs, the Doberman breed has incredible strength and remarkable endurance. They may have started out as guard dogs for rural tax collectors, but today's Dobermans can find work in a number of occupations, including police and military work, search and rescue, airport and dock work, and guard dogs. Additionally,

Dobermans are gentle and highly intuitive, which makes them ideal for use as therapy dogs, emotional support dogs, and leader dogs.

Your Doberman will quickly become a loyal and loveable member of your family. Life with a Doberman means lots of activity, lots of exercise, lots of love, and lots of big, slobbery kisses. Enjoy!

Your Trusted Doberman Pinscher Resource List

F or additional information about Doberman Pinschers and resources to help you find a reputable breeder in your region, here are some reputable breeders and rescue organizations, listed by location. This resource list should provide you a starting point for your search to find your new best friend and companion…your new Doberman Pinscher.

Doberman Pinscher Breeders in the United States

Canis -Maximus
http://canis-maximus.com
Virginia

Beshara Kennels
https://www.besharakennels.com
Jacksonville, Florida

Britton Farms
http://www.brittonfarmsdobermans.com/
Atlanta, Missouri

Dagobah Dobermans
http://www.dagobahdobermans.com/
Freehold, New York

Sierra Dobie Farms
http://www.sierradobiefarms.com/
Memphis, Tennessee

House of Hoytt
http://hoytt.com/
Dandridge, Tennessee

World Champion Unique Dobermans
https://www.uniquedobermans.com/
Bend, Oregon

Foxfire Dobermans
http://www.foxfiredobermans.com/
Sunny Valley, Oregon

Cambria Dobes
http://www.cambriadobes.com/
Millsap, Texas

Doberman Pinscher Breeders in Canada

Tri-Pinscher
https://www.tri-pinscher.com/
Leduc, Alberta

Hilltop Haven Dobermans
http://www.hilltophavendobermanns.ca/
Thunder Bay, Ontario

Dobereich Kennel
http://www.dobereich.com
Belwood, Ontario

Wrath Liberator
https://www.wrathliberator.com/
Harley, Ontario

Gate House Dobermans
https://gatehousedobermans.com/
Owens Sound, Ontario

Erobern Dobermans
http://www.eroberndobermans.com/
Winnipeg, Manitoba

Roulettes Dobermans
https://www.roulettesdobermans.com/
British Columbia

Doberman Pinscher Breeders in the U.K.

Ariaur Dobermanns
http://www.aritaur.co.uk/
Staffordshire, West Midlands

Tegrarado Dobermanns
http://www.tegratadobermanns.com/
London

Nolatari Dobermanns
http://www.nolataridobermanns.co.uk/
Manchester

Jojavik Dobermanns
http://jojavik.com
Foxburrows

Jodaseen Dobermanns
http://jodaseendobermanns.co.uk/
Whitby, North Yorkshire

Doberman Pinscher Rescue Groups in the United States

Doberman Pinscher Club of America
https://www.dpca.org/rescue/
chapters across the country

Dobies and Little Paws Rescue
http://www.dobiesandlittlepawsrescue.org/
Fillmore, California

Midwest Doberman Rescue
http://www.midwestdobermanrescuestl.org/
St. Louis, Missouri

Illinois Doberman Rescue
http://www.ildoberescue.com
Barrington, Illinois

Doberman Rescue Unlimited
http://www.dru.org/
Sandown, New Hampshire

Distinguished Doberman Rescue
http://www.ddrinc.net/
Moon Township, Pennsylvania

Hand Me Down Dobies
http://www.hmdd.org/
Lewis Center, Ohio

Doberman Rescue of North Texas
http://www.dobermanrescue.org/
Grand Prairie, Texas

Doberman Pinscher Rescue Groups in Canada

Doberman Rescue Ontario
http://doberescue.wixsite.com/dobermanrescue
Tottenham, Ontario

Doberman Pinscher Rescue Groups in the U.K.

Dobermann Rescue Ltd
https://www.dobermann-rescue.co.uk/
Wickford, Essex

Doberman Rehoming Association
http://dobermannrehome.co.uk/
Guildford, Surrey

Dobermanns in Need
https://www.dobermannsinneed.org/
South East England

19285794R00069

Made in the USA
San Bernardino, CA
22 December 2018